John Nicholson

Folk lore of East Yorkshire

John Nicholson

Folk lore of East Yorkshire

ISBN/EAN: 9783744778657

Printed in Europe, USA, Canada, Australia, Japan

Cover: Foto ©Thomas Meinert / pixelio.de

More available books at **www.hansebooks.com**

OF

EAST YORKSHIRE.

BY

JOHN NICHOLSON,

Author of "Folk Moots," "Beacons of East Yorkshire,"
"Folk Speech of East Yorkshire," &c.

(HON. LIBRARIAN HULL LITERARY CLUB).

LONDON: SIMPKIN, MARSHALL, HAMILTON, KENT, & CO.
HULL: A. BROWN & SONS, SAVILE STREET.
DRIFFIELD: T. HOLDERNESS, "OBSERVER" OFFICE.

1890.

DRIFFIELD :
PRINTED BY THOMAS HOLDERNESS,
MIDDLE STREET.

TO

ANDREW LANG, Esq., M.A.,

PRESIDENT OF THE FOLK LORE SOCIETY,
1890,

THIS VOLUME IS,

BY PERMISSION,

RESPECTFULLY DEDICATED

BY THE AUTHOR.

Forewords.

THE learning of the common folk, acquired by tradition, experience, or observation, and epitomised under the comprehensive title of Folk Lore, has, in these late years, received much attention, and its study has been prosecuted with due diligence and increasing interest. Learning and culture have given their invaluable aid, and scholars have traversed the treasures of the past, and have shewn us that the hoary antiquity of the Pyramids is not whiter than that which is borne by some of our nursery tales ; that many of these tales are world wide ; and that old customs, speech, and beliefs, linger with a tenacity which is difficult to loosen. The superstitious Welsh miners in the Morfa Colliery,* who caused a special examination of the pit to be made, in consequence of "spirits and noises and slamming of doors," previous to the disastrous explosion, are but typical of the great mass of people whose lives are more governed by folk lore than by book lore.

* Vide Daily Papers, April, 1890.

An Icelandic Sága tells of a man who, standing at his cottage door, saw some souls pass through the air. Among them he recognised his own, and had scarcely time to relate the incident before he died. Very many similar stories— stories not ancient, but very modern—are current to-day among the old folks. Here is one. A man went on St. Mark's Eve to watch in the church porch, where he saw enter the church the shades of several he knew, followed by some mysterious unknown forms, carrying a coffin. He endeavoured to see the features of the corpse, but was unable to do so; though, in answer to his earnest longing, a whisper came through the quiet midnight air, "'Tis yourself!" He went home, filled with fatal fear, took to his bed and died.

The appearance of the wraith or form of the deceased is still as firmly believed to be a sign of death as it was in the days of Olaf; and though the bah-gest,* with its eyes "as big as saucers," has ceased its terrifying rambles, and its growlings are no longer heard round the house of the doomed one, the howling of the yard dog has taken its place as an omen of death.

The ancient belief that the spirit requires space or room to pass still receives credence; for when a person is dying a window or door is opened in order that the spirit may pass away easily. One of the most vivid recollections of my boyhood is the death-bed of a younger brother. On a low bed, near a corner of the room, lay the poor little fellow whose life was rapidly ebbing. By the bedside sat my aged grandmother, silently praying, and the only sounds in the room were the laboured breathing of the dying boy and the smothered sobs of the assembled relatives; and as the end drew near my grandmother directed that a door leading into another room should be opened, and that room was ever afterwards associated with ghosts and spirits.

When the gods of our idolatrous forefathers, the hardy

* bear-ghost.

Norsemen, were dethroned from their seat of honour, by a change of faith, they were not deprived of power. They became devils, evil spirits, and ghosts, and maybe they exercised a more marked influence thereby. So Thor, with his mighty mallet, becomes the brigg-builder at Filey,* and the loss and recovery of his hammer is but the echo of a story from the Prose Edda.† The recovery in both legends is achieved by diving downwards.

Thor, whose name in Thursday is constantly on our lips, was he who threw thunder-bolts, as his car rumbled over the storm clouds; and thunder-bolts are very real to the rustic to-day, for he can pick them up in the fields, and they can have fallen only from the clouds.‡

When the Northman beheld the Northern Lights shooting athwart the wintry sky, and making the dark night splendid with brilliant streamers, his god Thor was abroad, doing battle on his behalf with the giants, for the gorgeous flaming signs were the beard of his divinity. The Thor has gone, given place to the "White Christ," but these lights are still the sign of war §—war more devilish than divine.

Red is the sacred colour. Thor's beard was red, and this doubtless led to the ascription of red hair to the betrayer Judas. The scarlet ibis is sacred to the Egyptians, the red-breast to English boys, and the rowan tree probably owes much of its ascribed virtue to its crimson berries.

Freyja, the goddess of love and purity in the Norse Mythology, whose name we have embalmed in the day-name Friday, was looked up to with love and adoration. "To that love and adoration, during the Middle Ages, one woman, transfigured into a divine shape, succeeded by a sort of natural right, and round the Virgin Mary's blessed head a halo of lovely tales of divine help, beams with soft radiance as a crown bequeathed to her by the ancient goddesses. Flowers and plants bear her name. In England, one of our

* p. 62.　　† p. 157.　　‡ p. 45.　　§ p. 45.

commonest and prettiest insects is still called after her, but which belonged to Freyja, the heathen 'Lady,' long before the western nations had learned to adore the name of the mother of Jesus." * If Thor has become the devil; if Bragi, the god of eloquence, has degenerated into *brag*; and Oegir, the sea-god, into an *ogre* to terrify children, or into the tidal wave (egir) of the Humber, it may be that Freyja has become the ghost or spirit common to the whole Riding. At Skipsea, at Cherry Burton, at Leven, at Brantinghamthorpe, and at other places, a headless white lady still affrights the traveller.

The carrying of a plough in procession on Plough Monday is probably a relic of the Miracle Plays of the Middle Ages, or a trace of some early worship or guild procession; the breaking of a plate at a wedding typical of the wholesale destruction attendant on a similar ceremony in Germany; the Pancake Bell a relic of the Shriving Bell; and the Death Bell the representative of the old Passing Bell, whose tones drove away the evil spirits lying in wait for the departing soul, which thus had a safe journey heavenwards.

Many of the tumuli or grave mounds on the Wolds are called "Fairy Hills," and the legend respecting Willy How † possesses features not unlike the following, taken from the *Story of Burnt Njal* :—"They cast a cairn over Gunnar, and made him sit upright in the cairn. Now this token happened at Liðend, that the neatherd and the waiting maid were driving cattle by Gunnar's cairn. They thought that he was merry, and that he was singing inside the cairn.

Now those two, Skarphedinn and Hogni, were out of doors one evening by Gunnar's cairn on the south side. The moon and stars were shining clear and bright, but every now and then the clouds drove over them. Then all at once they saw the cairn standing open, and lo! Gunnar had turned himself in the cairn and looked at the moon. They thought they

* Dr. Dasent's *Norse Tales*, li.   † p. 83.

saw four lights burning in the cairn, and none of them threw a shadow. They saw that Gunnar was merry, and he wore a joyful face. He sang a song, and so loud that it might have been heard though they had been further off.

> He that lavished rings in largesse,
>   When the fights' red rain-drops fell,
> Bright of face, with heart-strings hardy,
>   Hogni's father met his fate ;
> Then his brow with helmet shrouding,
>   Bearing battle shield, he spake,
> ' I will die the prop of battle,
>   Sooner die than yield an inch,
> Yes, sooner die than yield an inch.' "

After that the cairn was shut up again.

The hand-clasp on the conclusion of a bargain * is a very old custom as the following extract from the *Story of Burnt Njal* shews :—" Then Hrut held his peace some little while, and afterwards he stood up and said to Oswif—' Take now my hand in handsel as a token that thou lettest the suit drop.' So Oswif stood up and said—' This is not an atonement on equal terms when thy brother utters the award, but still thou (speaking to Hrut) hast behaved so well about it that I trust thee thoroughly to make it.' Then he stood up and took Hauskuld's hand, and came to an atonement in the matter."

The rate of progress to-day is almost electrical in its velocity. Many manners, customs, and beliefs are only memories, and may soon cease to be that, and their preservation is necessary, as a detail, to complete the full picture of the past, of which the present is the glorious outcome. We ought no more to despise those beliefs and doings of the past, than ought the butterfly to repudiate the crawling worm from which it came. We may laugh in scorn

* p. 30.

at some of the things to which our grandfathers gave credence, but our laugh should be one of joy that we are free from the bondage which bound them.

Hull Literary Club.   J. NICHOLSON.
    26. IV. 90.

Contents.

Illustrations.

Roll Call of Helpers,

to whom the author tenders his thanks for services and information, many and valuable.

Andrews, William, Esq., F.R.H.S., Hull. Author of *Curiosities of the Church*, &c.

Bainton, T., Esq., Arram Hall, Seaton.

Boodie, J., Esq., Hull.

Browne, J. Esq., Bridlington Quay. Author of *William Bradley*, &c.

Cole, Rev. E. M., M.A., Wetwang. Author of *Geological Rambles*, &c.

Collins, Rev. W. H., M.A., York.

Cooper, Rev. A. N., Filey.

Harman, Matthew, Esq., Scarbro'. Author of *Poetic Buds*, &c.

Holderness, Thos., Esq., Driffield. Author of *The Battle of Brunanburh*.

Jones, G. J., Esq., Malton.

Maddock, Rev. H. E., M.A., Patrington.

Morris, Rev. M. C. F., Newton-on-Ouse.

Page, W. G. B., Esq., Royal Institution, Hull.

Ross, Fred, Esq., F.R.H.S., London. Author of *Celebrities of the Yorkshire Wolds*.

Sawden, Miss Clara, Lissett.

Souter, W., Esq., Hedon.

Stork, the late James, Esq., Skipsea.

Topham, Miss Lizzie, High Bonwick.

Turner, J. Horsfall, Esq., Idel.   Editor of *Yorkshire Notes and Queries.*

Turner, T. E., Esq., Walkergate, Beverley.

Turner, T., Junr., Esq., Holgate, York.

Vyvyan, Rev. Hy., M.A., York.

Wildridge, T. Tindall, Esq., Beverley.   Author of *Old and New Hull,* &c.

Wood, Dr. R., Medical Officer of Health, Driffield.

Abbreviations and List of Works Consulted.

ANDERSON. "The Sailor; a Poem," by Edward Anderson. Driffield, 1878.

ANDREWS. "Curious Epitaphs," by William Andrews, F.R.H.S. London, 1883.

BEST. "Rural Economy in Yorkshire, in 1641." Surtees Society, 1857.

DASENT. "Popular Tales from the Norse," by Geo. Webbe Dasent, D.C.L. Edinburgh, 1859.

HAZLITT. "English Proverbs," by W. Carew Hazlitt. London, 1882.

HENDERSON. "Folk Lore of the Northern Counties," by Wm. Henderson. Folk Lore Society, 1879.

HOLD. GLOSS. "A Glossary of Words used in Holderness," by T. Holderness, F. Ross, and R. Stead. English Dialect Society. London, 1877.

COX. "The Mythology of the Aryan Nations," by the Rev. Sir George W. Cox, Bart., M.A. London, 1882.

PARKINSON. "Yorkshire Legends and Traditions," by Rev. Thos. Parkinson, F.R.H.S. London, 1888.

TWYFORD AND GRIFFITH. "Records of York Castle,"
          London, 1880.

WESLEY.   "Primitive Physic," by John Wesley, M.A.

WILDRIDGE. "Holderness and Hullshire Gleanings," by T.
          Tindall Wildridge.   Hull, 1886.

The columns and pages of newspapers and magazines have
yielded a considerable harvest.   Among them may be
mentioned :—*Leeds Mercury Supplement, Yorkshire Weekly
Post, Notes and Queries, Yorkshire Notes and Queries,
Lincolnshire Notes and Queries, Folk Lore Journal,* &c.

FOLK LORE OF EAST YORKSHIRE.

CHAPTER I.

Ceremonial Customs.

UNDER this title will be treated all that pertains to birth, baptism, and christening; to weddings, death, and burial.

BIRTH.

It is important that the exact time of birth be noted, so that when the wise man is consulted concerning the future of the infant, he may be able to correctly assign the influence of the planets which were in conjunction or in opposition at the time of birth. If the child be born with a caul, this must be carefully preserved, for, by some subtle occult influence, it will notify the original owner's death, though he may be far away. A caul, which had been large and dry for years, has been known to grow damp and shrivel up, when its first owner died abroad.

When a child is born, it is no uncommon thing to have

A

an unlimited supply of liquor in the house, so that all visitors may drink to the health of the little stranger. The happy father stands "treats" innumerable to congratulating friends, and finally invites a few choice spirits to a carousal, to "wet bayne heead."

BAPTISM.

For baptism, the infant must be dressed in white, like a bride, and the water sprinkled by the clergyman on its little face must not be wiped off, but must dry on. If the child make no noise when the cold water drops on its face, it is considered an unlucky omen; but this does not often happen, and some children would be very lucky if noise would bring such a fortunate result.

In country districts, infants are often baptised at home, but all christenings must be done at the church. The christening is often deferred until the general and customary gathering of friends, at feast or fair time, renders the ceremony more gratifying and imposing. After leaving the church the united company have a grand feast, followed by abundance of gin, &c., and, in the days anterior to tea and temperance, many drunken disgraceful scenes formed a serious blot on our village life.

Old-fashioned nurses still insist on babies wearing a closely-fitting cap for the first twelve weeks, as was the custom when the said nurses were children in arms.

VISITS.

When the baby first visits any house it is considered the proper thing to present it with a box or bundle of matches, an egg, some salt in a piece of paper, and a piece of money, so that it may never lack light, food, friendship, nor money, during its life. In childhood, when the child puts on any new article of dress, containing a pocket, it is usual to put therein a piece of money, to "hansel" it, and a small present of money is invariably given by friends to whom the dress is shewn. Such money, however, is not to be frivolously spent, but is to be saved in the little "thrif-box," which stands on the chimney-piece, until enough is accumulated to buy something useful.

MARRIAGE.

On the wedding day, the bride is to be congratulated if the morning be bright and fine. Green is an unlucky colour, so it finds no place in her dress, and she ought not to see the bridegroom that morning, until they meet in church. After the ceremony, as they emerge from the sacred building, arm in arm, guns are fired to celebrate the event: even the old women find some ancient flint-lock, horse-pistol, or blunderbuss, which they discharge, with the muzzle resting on the window sill. Near the house in which the bridal feast is spread, stand three or four men with guns crammed to the muzzle with feathers, and, as the party passes them, the guns are discharged, and the air is filled with falling feathers, thereby betokening a wish that nothing harder may ever fall on the happy pair. When the party arrives at the house, a plate full of small pieces of bridecake is given to the bridegroom, who throws the plate and its contents over the bride's head into the roadway, where the children scramble for the pieces. If the plate be not broken by the fall, some friend of the newly-married pair immediately seizes it, and stamps on it, for good luck is proportional to the number of bits.

In the evening, a race is run by men for a broad piece of ribbon, the ribbon being as carefully provided by the bride as the ring by the bridegroom, and the winner of the race has the privilege of kissing the bride, the ribbon being his passport. Boys also run races for sweets, nuts, and pence.

This race for the ribbon is considered such an institution, that, when an attempt was made on one occasion to discontinue the practice, quite a disturbance was created, and eventually a race was run for a knot of black tape, which was locally known as "Stingy Tom Ribbon."

The following, from Best's *Rural Economy* * (p. 116) bears on this subject of marriage :—"Concerninge our Fashions att our Country Weddinges. Usually the young man's father or hee himselfe writes to the father of the maid to knowe if hee shall bee welcome to the howse, if hee shall have his furtherance if hee come in such a way, or howe hee liketh of the notion; then if hee pretend any excuse onely thankinge him for his good will, then that is as good as a denyall. If the notion bee thought well of and imbraced, then the yonge man gooth perhapps twice to see how the mayd standeth affeckted; then if hee see that shee bee tractable and that her inclination is towards him then the third time that hee visiteth, hee perhapps giveth her a tenne shillinge peece of gold or a ringe of that price; or perhapps a twenty shillinge peece or a ringe of that price; then the next time, or next after that, a payr of gloves of 6s. 8d. or 10s. a payre; and after that each other time some conceited toy or novelty of less value. They visite usually every three weekes or a moneth and are usually halfe a yeare or very neare from the first going to the conclusion. Soo soone as the younge folkes are agreed and contracted, then the father of the mayd carryeth her over to the younge man's howse, to see howe they like of all, and there doth the younge man's father meete them to treate of a dower, and likewise of a joynture or feoffment for the woman; and then doe they allsoo appointe and sette downe the day of marriage, which may perhapps bee aboute a fortnight or three weekes after, and in that time doe they gette made the weddinge cloathes, and make provision against the weddinge dinner, which is usually att the mayds father's. Theyre use is to buy gloves to give to each of theyre friends a payre on that day; the man should bee att the cost for them; but sometimes the man gives gloves to the men, and the woman to the women, or else hee to her friends and shee to his; they give them that morninge when they are allmost ready to goe to church to be marryed. Then soe soone as the bride is tyred and that they are ready to goe forthe, the bridegroome comes and takes her by the hand and sayth, "Mistris, I hope you are willinge" or else kisseth her before them and then followeth her father out of the doores; then one of the bridegroome his men ushereth the bride and goes foremost, and the rest of the younge men usher each of them a mayd to church. The bridegroome and the bride's brothers or freinds tende att dinner; hee perhapps fetcheth her hoame to his howse aboute a moneth after and the portion is paide that morninge that she goes away. When the younge man comes to fetch away his bride some of his best freinds and younge men his neighbours, come alonge with him, and others perhapps meete them in the way and then is there the same jollity att his howse, for they perhapps have love wine ready to give to the company when they light, then a dinner, supper, and breakfast, next day."

DEATH.

When, by holding a hand glass to the mouth, it has been ascertained that death has taken place, the door or window of the room is opened to allow the spirit to pass out easily, and if, owing to the presence of pigeon's feathers in the bed, the death has been so hard that the poor creature has been lifted in the sheet off the bed on to the floor, the body is returned to the bedstead and laid out. All the looking glasses in the house are either turned to the wall or covered up, and the clocks stopped.

One of the attendants carries the news to the sexton, who, for a small fee, tolls the death bell. At the conclusion of such tolling, after a short pause, he gives nine strokes for a child, thirteen for a woman, and fifteen for a man. These numbers vary in nearly every district. At Patrington, where the church has five bells, they are tolled once round (five strokes) for a child; twice round (ten strokes) for a woman;

and thrice round (fifteen strokes) for a man. The bell is also tolled on the evening before the funeral, and at one o'clock on the day of the burial. The formation of cemeteries has rendered the custom obsolete in many districts, as an old sexton said "It's only auld standards* at wants it noo!"

BIDDING.

One or two women go round to neighbours, friends, and relatives, telling them of the death, and asking them to attend the funeral. This asking is termed "bidding," and it is considered an honour to be "bid," while the neglect or oversight of not "bidding" has been known to cause family feuds and disagreements, lasting perhaps for years.

BURIAL.

After the corpse has been laid out it must be constantly watched till buried, and at night a light is kept burning in the room. Lamps have almost superseded candles, but in olden time when the candle required snuffing, it was only a very bold person who could enter alone to perform that necessary operation. On the night before the funeral a few friends would assemble for a night wake (watch), and were expected to leave when the newly-lighted candle had burned into the socket. There was the parish clerk, who was also a joiner and undertaker, and who could sing a bit of all parts, and start tunes; the blacksmith, who sang bass, and whose swarthy face, bright from recent application of soap, was eclipsed by the scarlet kerchief twisted round his neck; the "reet" (wright) had doffed the white apron which is usually twisted round his waist, and appeared in a dark coat that contrasted strangely with his corduroys, worn sleek and smooth at the knees and round the slit for his two-foot rule. He sang seconds. The old schoolmaster, who had taught the deceased, took off his old beaver hat as he entered, and

* Standards—Standers, those of old standing. Compare drunk-ards, cow-ards, &c.

carefully brushed it ere he put it in the broad window-seat, and, taking off a black silk scarf, displayed the only white collar in the room. His voice was tremulous with age and emotion, when they all joined in singing the favourite hymns of the deceased, which hymns had been chosen only a few hours before death.

These, with the nearest relatives of the departed one, formed the most important points in the large semi-circle round the fire, while behind, between, and before, stood, kneeled, or crouched, sorrowing friends and relatives, old and young, upon whose tear-stained faces the fire-light flickered and danced, and which also made fantastic shadows on the walls and ceiling.

After the hymns have been sung and reminiscences related, the women take the children home to bed, and the elders stay awhile, to smoke their long clay pipes and taste the home-brewed ale, but by and by these go too, and only the nearest relatives are left.

It is related that on one occasion, after the appearance of the gin bottle on the table, the bad blood, which had previously existed between the brothers of a certain family, exhibited itself in quarrelling and fighting. As the noise increased, some of the friends returned, and two of them, more venturesome than the rest, went to the room in which the corpse lay, took it, all swathed in flannel as it was, carried it to the door of the room where the disturbance was, knocked loudly at the door and then ran away. When one of the brothers opened the door, and they saw the corpse there, they were sobered instantly, believing that their wicked behaviour had actually brought their poor old mother out of her coffin, to put a stop to their unseemly conduct.

Before the coffin lid is screwed down, the class tickets, hymn book, or bible, are placed with the corpse, and flowers strewn over all. Bearers of similar age and of the same sex as the deceased, carry the body to the grave-yard, favourite

hymns being sung the whole way, and when the church-yard
gate is reached, the men singers halt, form a ring, and stand
singing until the rest have passed in, when they too fall in
and bring up the rear.

Before leaving the house for the grave-yard, the mourners
have refreshment served to them—cheese, spice-bread, and
beer for the men; biscuits and wine, both home-made, for
the women. On returning to the house, a funeral feast is
prepared, the like of which is only seen at these times. One
house will not always contain the guests, and the adjoining
houses are willingly lent for the occasion. Sometimes, however, a school-room is engaged, wherein all can sit down
together, instead of having two or three "sittings down."
These feasts are remembered by the greatness of the provision
made for them, and a strong rivalry once existed, happily
dying out, by which friends strove to excel each other ; and
the expense was so great that families were impoverished for
years.

At the funeral of a maiden, a pair of white gloves used to
be carried at the head of the procession, by a girl about the
same age and as much like the deceased as possible, and
these gloves were afterwards hung up in the church, near to
the place usually occupied by the departed one. The gloves
bore the maiden's name, age, and date of death, and the
bearers of such were dressed all in white. On the Sunday
following the funeral, all friends and relatives met at the
church or other place of worship, dressed in mourning, and
special reference to the departed one was generally made in
the sermon, and the favourite hymns sung again. After this
day, the black dress, which had been donned as a token of
respect, is discarded by all save relations and the most
intimate friends.

Black kid gloves, black hat-bands, and black silk scarves,
used to be provided for all the officials who were invited,
and many a careful housewife has got a splendid silk dress

out of the scarves obtained by her husband and sons. At the funeral of a woman a white shawl formed a proper article of mourning.

Of church officials, the dog "nauper" (whipper) is now obsolete, but it was customary for him to head the funeral procession, with his rod of office decorated with a black crape bow.

CHAPTER II.

ffestival Customs.

BEFORE the days of Friendly Societies and Odd Fellows, the Provident Sick and Benefit Clubs took their place, and the anniversaries of those clubs formed Club Feasts, which, in villages that had no fair, was a day of sport and merriment. A club of this kind in Beverley was known as the Duck and Green Peas Club, because these delicacies formed the chief item in the *menu* of their club dinner. The Etton Club Feast was moveable from place to place, to suit the convenience of its widely-scattered members.

These Club Feasts and pleasure feasts and races, though obsolete in many villages, are still celebrated, perhaps with diminished glory, but yet with enough rejoicing to form a red-letter day in the quiet, uneventful, rural life of our villages.

With banners flying, and headed by a brass band, the members of the club proceed in procession to the Church, and, after the service, return to the village inn, where ample justice is done to the splendid repast, which fully sustains the reputation of mine host of the Jolly Waggoners. On the village green, but more particularly in the neighbourhood of the inn already mentioned, are numerous stalls of sweets and toys, shows of things rare and wonderful, shooting galleries, ballad singers, that remind one of the skalds of our

Norse forefathers, and here a group of old men, that are mourning the lack of excitement since they can have no cock-fighting, bull-baiting, or badger-baiting.

Fairs, which were once important, have died a natural death. Railways have diverted traffic, and annihilated distance, so that instead of having to wait weeks or months for the fair to supply a market, or meet a demand, a few hours railway journey will do all that is required. Some fairs, chiefly for the sale of cattle, horses, sheep, &c., are still held, and form a suitable opportunity for the meeting of friends and relations, for whose benefit the best obtainable is provided ; and the day, after the transaction of business, is given to merriment and sports. Before Sunday sports were abolished, football was played after morning service, on the feast Sunday, the parson frequently "kicking off."

At Feast time, in the olden days, open house was kept by nearly every one : you could scarcely get to the wrong house, for wherever you went you were welcome. Cheesecakes form the common fare, though brandy-snap is the favourite at Hull, and currant cakes or spice loaves, backed by a huge lump of cheese, are as freely given as taken. Friends give each other small presents called "fairings."

For parties, a large round cake, called matrimony cake, having a layer of currants between two layers of pastry, is covered with sugar, then cut into as many pieces as there are persons at the feast. Into one piece would be placed a silver coin ; in another a wedding ring, borrowed for the occasion from the hostess ; in a third, a button. Those to whom the money fell were to be rich ; the receiver of the ring was to be married soon ; while the luckless wight whose piece contained the button was to die in single blessedness.

In some parts of Holderness, no birthday is considered properly celebrated unless a birthday cake is made, of ten or twelve alternate layers of paste and currants, with sugar spread on the top. This cake is cut up at the birthday tea.

Though this style of cake is becoming obsolete, a currant cake is the common fare for birthdays.

On Ash Wednesday the game of tut-ball was indulged in, or else the non-players would be sure to fall sick in the harvest time; and on Palm Sunday, the catkins of the willow, called palms, are carried in the hand, and used for domestic decoration. At Filey, figs were once eaten on Palm Sunday, but the custom is now obsolete.

Passion Sunday, the fifth Sunday in Lent, is called Carlin Sunday, the proper fare for that day being grey peas, steeped over night in water, and fried in butter or fat. At the proper season, we used to have papers and pockets full of these delicacies, for they were delicious; and even this year (1889) I have seen them for sale in shops in Hull at a half-penny a half-pint glassfull.

At Easter, boys and girls try to catch each other by the ankles to trip one another up, or "leg them down" as they say. Hence Easter Monday is known as "Leggin Day;" but, if you trip any one up at any time, you offer as excuse "It's Leggin Day ti-day!"

The Monday before Shrove Tuesday is called Collop Monday, and it is customary to have a dish of eggs and bacon for dinner on that day. On Shrove Tuesday (Pancake Tuesday) pancakes are provided, and in some places the Pancake bell is rung at eleven o'clock in the morning, when the children expect to be allowed to leave school, and have a half-holiday, in which to play games with ball. As "keppin" (catching) balls, is the favourite game, the day is called Keppin Day. Another game also gave its name to this day. Men and youths used to have hard-boiled eggs, which they "throwled" (rolled) on the grass. The eggs were dyed, and he whose egg rolled the farthest or longest, was the winner. So Shrove Tuesday was called Throwl-egg-day.

The following rhyme includes these and other days.

> Egg and Collop Monda'
> Pancake 'Tuesda'
> Ash Wednesda'
> Bloody Thursda' *
> Lang Frida 'll nivver be deean
> Then hey for Setherda' eftherneean.

An old couplet, by which the Lenten Sundays were distinguished, was :—

> "Tid, mid, and miseray,
> Carlin, paum, and good feeast day."

It is suggested that Tid is from Te Deum ; Mid for middle ; Miseray from miserere ; Carlin from carlins (q.v.) ; Paum from palm ; Good Feast day being Easter Sunday.

Cole's *History of Filey* says that an Easter custom prevails there of young men taking the shoes of the females, and of the females retaliating by taking the hats of the men next day. All the articles are redeemed on a subsequent evening, when they all meet at one of the inns and finish by a supper.

The first day of April being dedicated to All Fools, many attempts, often successful, are made to increase the ranks of the foolish All. A very common way is to send a guileless youth to the shoemaker's for some stirrup-oil, which is given to him across his back ; the said stirrup being the leather band used by shoemakers to hold their work firmly on their knee. Once a boy was sent on this day, to a bookseller's shop, in Bridlington, for "The Life of Adam's grandfather ;" though a pennyworth of pigeon's milk from the chemist's is a favourite device.

On the first of May, May "geslins" (goslings) are made similarly to April fools ; but on both days it is not allowable

* The Thursday before Good Friday.

to continue the practice after mid-day.   If it were done, the
retort would be :—

> " Twelve o'clock is past and gone,
>   So you're a fool for making one."

During the days of spring, boys busily "bird nest" (seek
nests), and lay up a store of eggs for the 29th of May, Royal
Oak Day, or Mobbing day.   These eggs are expended by
being thrown at other boys, but all boys who carry a sprig
of Royal oak, not dog-oak, either in their cap or coat, are free
from molestation.   Not only wild birds' eggs, but the eggs of
hens and ducks are used to "mob" (pelt) with, and the
older and more unsavoury the eggs are the better are they
liked—by the thrower.

On this day school children sing :—

> " The twenty-ninth of May,
>   Royal Oak Day,
>   If you don't give us a holiday,
>   We'll all run away."

No nesting is done after this day.

Whit Sunday is the day on which people appear in new
clothes.   The very poorest will try to have something, if
not everything, new.   How differently our girls are dressed
now to what they used to be, in low shoes with ankle straps
or crossed elastic, white stockings, white dresses with short
sleeves, a light shawl, and a large hat or white hood.

It used to be a custom to make a bonfire on mid-summer
eve, but the practice appears to have been discontinued for
many years.

In the old mowing days, when the standing corn was laid
low by scythes, it was considered an eventful and honourable
thing to give the finishing strokes.   Any visitor who could
handle a scythe was allowed to do it, the last falling straws

being hailed with cheers, and probably the visitor paid his "footing" for the operation.

When the last load of corn is "led" into the "staggath" (stackyard) the good wife scrambles nuts and apples among the expectant children, who have come in with the last wagon. The men and children sing a song which varies in different districts. The following rhyme was once common about Hornsea :—

> " We hev her, we hev her,
>   A coo iv a tether ;
> At oor toon end,
>   A yow an a lamb,
> A pot an a pan,
>   May we get seeaf in,
> Wiv oor hahvest yam,
>   Wiv a sup o' good yal,
> An sum hawpence ti spend."

The harvest is all gathered in and safely housed or thatched ; hedges have been cut down ; and the stubble in the fields, together with thorns, form material for a great bonfire. For weeks the boys have been gathering stores of fuel, secretly, and in fear of the policeman ; and all spare pence have been expended on gunpowder or fireworks, also done secretly and in fear of the maternal slipper, if they bring such dangerous stuff into the house.

Now the day has arrived, and the hour, and as soon as eleven o'clock has struck the eldest apprentice in the village goes to the church "to put the bell in," that is, to ring the bell, and at the sound the children are dismissed from school, the apprentices leave work, and sport is the order of the day.

A farmer has placed one of his fields at the disposal of the plotters, and given a cartload of straw and another of thorns to help in providing fuel for a bonfire. With shout and laughter, additional fuel is brought by the boys, each large

arrival being hailed with joyous peals of merriment; while
the church bells ring all the time, now steadily, now clashing
together, now in straggling fitful strokes, as the ringers tire,
or as some amateur handles the rope.

Evening has now come, and, amid great excitement,
matches are applied in several places to the huge pile; and,
as the dense smoke gives place to flickering flames, the
people cheer lustily, while pistols and guns are discharged,
and squibs and crackers startle and terrify the timorous, and
the children dance and shout :—

> Gunpowder plot,
> Shall never be forgot,
> So long as Old England
> Stands on its spot.

Youths have old besoms, dipped in tar, which they kindle
at the bonfire, and they rush about swinging the blazing
torches above their heads; and the bells tell of the unsteady
hands that hold the ropes, for much strong ale has been
taken into the belfry during the day.

So the night wears on; the last rocket has ascended
bright and glorious, and the charred stick now lies on the
ground; the last shot has been fired; the ringers have left
the belfry, and their drunken shouts have died away; the
children have been taken home to bed; the fire burns low,
and as a tiny flame now and then flickers into sight and
quickly disappears, the pale thin smoke forms a column in
the calm air, that looks almost spectral in the dim moonlight.

On the eve of the 5th of November youths used to go
round the village and strike the doors of the cottages with
babbles—leather bags each having a stone inside and a string
attached. For these lively proclivities, they received few
blessings, many forcible words, and sometimes a sound
thrashing.

Martinmas time being over, some of the unhired men disguise themselves by dressing in motley garb. One will dress as a woman, and, carrying a besom, is known as Besom Bet; another having his hat and coat covered with strips of all kinds and colours of rags, has a "blether" (bladder) attached by a string to the end of a stick, and is called "Blether Dick;" the others adopt other devices, and, going from village to village, collect odd pence. Dick and Bet form the comic element, the former using his "blether" to maintain order, much to the amusement of the boys, who often get a sounding whack on their heads or backs. These "Ploo Lads" (Plough Boys) seldom have a plough with them, as they used to have, but execute a rude dance wherever they think there is gain.

I saw a band of these in Beverley, on the evening of Friday, the 13th of December, 1889, but their "get up" was not so good as I have seen. Often their disguise is so complete that at lonely houses they are rude and bold, demanding money or drink in such a way as to terrify the women who have been left at home. The writer has a vivid recollection of his mother keeping one of these fellows at bay with a sweeping brush, while he bolted the door to prevent any farther inroad.

About Christmas time, women or girls called Bezzlecup or Vesselcup women go from house to house, with two dolls in a box, representing the Virgin and Child. Instead of these dolls, on one occasion I saw a cup, like a prize cup, in the box. These women sing carols, of which one is :—

> "God bless the maisther of this hoose,
> An' mistheris also,
> Likewise the pretty childheren,
> That roond your table go.
> For now it is at Christmas time
> We travel far and near,
> So God bless you, an' send to you
> A Happy New Year."

B

At this season of the year shopkeepers are expected to make a present to their customers. With grocers, almanacks, often very beautiful and artistic, have superseded the coloured Christmas candle, and its accompaniments of plums for the Christmas pudding. On Christmas Eve this candle is lighted, and it burns in the post of honour, either in the middle of the table or on the mantel-piece, while the inmates of the cottage partake of "frumerty" (boiled wheat) sweetened with treacle and spices, and having spice bread and cheese therewith. During the day the Christmas "clog" (log) had been brought by the "wreet's" (wheel-wright's) apprentice, and he had a few coppers given to him as a "Christmas box." A small piece of last year's log, which has been carefully and purposely preserved, is now brought out, placed on the fire, and the new log laid on the top.

As the night advances, sounds of music fill the air—the flute, violin, cello, and other instruments, mingled with human voices, and, as they come nearer, the words of their carol can be distinguished—

> "While shepherds watched their flocks by night,
>   All seated on the ground;
> The angel of the Lord came down,
>   And glory shone around."

These are the "waits," and, though many of them go round for private and personal profit, the greater number use this ancient custom for charitable purposes, and collect money, either for distribution to the poor or to replenish some fund in connection with their place of worship. If for the latter purpose, after they have patrolled the principal streets and visited the influential members of their denomination, they will return to their schoolroom about midnight, to partake of a hot supper, bountifully provided by some of the ladies of their congregation.

In keeping with the hospitality of this season, hotels and inns provide a huge game pie for their customers, and none of the good things provided for this festive time are better than these pies, "standing pies" they are called, being nearly a foot high, and filled with the choicest morsels of hare, rabbit, pheasant, &c. Spice bread and cheese are also provided, and such ale as only the most seasoned toper can withstand.

On Christmas morning, boys come wishing you a merry Christmas, saying—

> " Ah wish yo' a merry Christmas
> An' a happy New Year,
> A pocket full o' money,
> An' a cellar full o' beer,
> Two fat pigs an' a new cauved coo,
> Misthress an' Maisther hoo di ya do,
> An' pleeas will yo' gi' ma a Christmas box,"

and expect to receive money in return. Many houses have three gifts, the first boy receiving a shilling, the second sixpence, the third threepence, and all who come afterwards receive nothing, being told they are too late. The giving of presents on this day is general, and children hang up their stockings over night, as a receptacle for such gifts as their friends bestow.

The Christmas joint, followed by plum pudding, is the best that can be provided. To this end, cattle have been fed, poultry, geese and turkeys, fattened, and hares, rabbits, and other game have hung in hundreds and thousands round the game dealers' shops. Churches, houses, and shops are decorated with evergreens, and the ladies of the house do not forget to suspend a bunch of mistletoe in some conspicuous place, easily accessible, under which a pleasant custom is indulged in, which will certainly never be allowed to become obsolete. Where the mistletoe plant cannot be obtained, a hoop covered with evergreens, and decorated with oranges and apples, bears the same name and carries the same privileges.

On the eve and night of Christmas Day, games are played, parties given, and the sport kept up until a late hour. One of the pleasantest recollections of childhood is the memory of forming one of a waggon load of young folks returning from a children's Christmas party, and singing carols and songs all the way home, making the midnight air re-echo with our shrill voices.

On New Year's Eve, the bells peal merrily until shortly before midnight, when a muffled peal is rung, and then a pause, which seems all the quieter after the ringing of the bells. The silence is broken by the striking of the midnight hour, which has been eagerly listened for at open windows and doors, and by groups of people in the street. The last stroke of the hour has scarcely ceased sounding, before the bells ring out a wild peal that makes the old church tower rock again, and the listening people offer mutual congratulations and good wishes.

Great importance is attached to the person who enters the house first in the New Year, and who is termed the "first foot, or lucky bird." The person must be dark and of the male sex. A story is told of a woman who went to her neighbours to borrow something on the morning of New Year's Day. She was the "first-foot," and could not be admitted until the husband of the house had gone out at the back door, and entered the house at the front door. A lady once told me that her sister came first to the door on New Year's morning, and that her mother was greatly troubled about it, and only admitted her daughter with great reluctance because of the wet inclement weather. The mother, herself, died in March of the same year, and that unlucky first foot was then looked upon as an omen of death.

After boys or men have been admitted as "lucky-bird,"

girls, often in bands of three or four, go from house to house wishing the inmates a Happy New Year, and receiving in return New Year Gifts. Poor widows receive donations from generous people, which help to alleviate the general distress of winter.

On New Year's day, it is a custom at Driffield for the boys of the town to assemble in the main street, go in disorderly rout to the shops of the chief tradesmen and, standing in the road before each shop, sing out :

> " Here we are at oor toon end,
> A shooldher o mutton, an a croon ti spend.
> Hip ! hip ! hooray !"

until some of the stock of the tradesman is thrown to them and scrambled for.

The Flambro' children, who run after the vehicles which convey visitors to and from their picturesque neighbourhood, have a variation of this rhyme—

> " Here we are at oor toon end,
> A bottle o' gin, and a croon ti spend.
> If ya hain't a penny, a hawp'ny 'll do ;
> If ya hain't a hawp'ny, God bless you !
> Hip ! hip ! hooray ! "

Fifty years ago, Kirkham Bird Fair used to be held on the bridge across the Derwent, connecting the East and North Ridings. Here, at two o'clock in the morning, on Trinity Monday, boys used to bring jackdaws, owls, rooks, starlings, &c., and "swap," (exchange or barter), or sell, the parapet of the bridge serving as a counter. The fair was over by daylight, and then drinking tents, booths, and stalls, made their appearance as prelude to a pleasure fair; but the day often ended in fisticuffs between the rivals of Malton and

Westow. There was an attempt to stop the Fair, when a new squire bought the Priory estate, but the boys just moved to the North Riding end of the bridge, and so moved out of his jurisdiction. The Fair is supposed to have had its origin in monastic times, by persons offering to supply the Abbey with poultry, and was held for many years close to the old cross in front of the Abbey gateway.

Best says, (p. 113). "On Munday in Whitsun-weeke there is a fayre at Little Driffield to which Nafferton and Lowthorpe men come with clubbs to keepe goode order and rule the faire; they have a piper to play before them, and the like doinges is att the latter Lady-day in harvest." The fair is still held but no piper or men with clubs to keep good order are there.

At Hedon, on Shrove Tuesday, all the apprentices, whose indentures terminated before the return of that day, used to assemble at the belfry of the church at 11 o'clock, and, in turn, toll the tenor bell for an hour. At the sound of the bell, all the housewives began the making of pancakes. The sexton got a small fee from each apprentice. This custom was discontinued in 1885.

Formerly a custom existed in the seaport town of Hull of whipping all the dogs that were found running about the streets on the 10th of October, and so common was the practice at one time, that every little street arab considered it his bounden duty to prepare a whip for any unlucky dog that might be seen wandering in the streets on that day.

A correspondent of *Notes and Queries* says that tradition assigns the following origin to the custom:— Previous to the suppression of the Monasteries in Hull, it was customary for the monks to provide liberally for the poor and wayfarers who visited the fair held annually on October 11th, and which still continues as a pleasure Fair on that day. Once while the good brothers were making the neces-

sary preparations, on the day previous to the fair, a dog
strolled into the larder, and on leaving, snatched up a piece
of meat and made off with it. The cooks instantly sounded
the alarm, and when the dog got into the street he was
pursued by the hungry expectants of the charity of the
monks, who were waiting outside the gates, and made to give
up the stolen joint. After this occurrence, whenever a dog
ventured to show his face during the annual feast preparations
he was invariably beaten off.

In days gone by, a similar custom was observed at York,
on St. Luke's Day, (Oct. 18), which from this circumstance
came to be popularly designated " Whip-Dog-Day." Tradition
asserts that centuries since, as a priest was celebrating mass,
on St. Luke's festival, in a church at York, he accidentally
dropped the host, after consecration, which was instantly
swallowed by a dog crouched under the altar. This act of
profanation caused the dog's death, and inaugurated a
persecution which was afterwards kept up on the anniversary
of the day.

On this same day, used to be held in Micklegate, York, a
fair called Old Dish Fair, because wooden dishes, bowls,
spoons, &c., were the chief wares. During the fair a strange
custom was observed. Four strong men, each supported by
another, carried two stangs, from which was suspended a
wooden ladle. Eight men to carry one ladle! It was supposed to represent the idea that the wooden articles required
much labour and yielded little profit.

Maudlin (Magdalen) Fair used to be held on the 2nd of
August, on the Magdalen Hill, Hedon, and was continued
several days on the market hill. As the Fair became of less
importance, the tenant of the field tried to prevent anyone
entering on the day appointed for the fair, and though
sometimes unsuccessful, by dint of bribing and giving a
shilling each to those desirous of entering, the fair was

finally abolished about 1860.   The following is a reprint of
a song, descriptive of the Fair in its best days :—

" Let Lords in their Bag Wigs, and Ladies in gause,
    At Court strut and stare, or at Balls seek applause,
Can such create envy, can aught give us care ?
    While pleasures invite us like Magdalen Fair.

No plotting ambition, no polish'd deceit,
    No patches or Paint, at this revel we meet ;
Our greetings are Blessings not purchas'd by wealth,
    The smile of content, and the Rose bloom of Health.

Maidens long wishing for this happy day,
    Pray old Father time to pass quickly away ;
To reach this gay scene, all contrivance they try,
    And those who can't get there—they sit down and cry.

Here Damsels all Beauty, enliven'd by Youth,
    With Eyes full of light'ning and Hearts full of truth ;
Impell'd by dame Nature in spite of their Dads,
    Parade in their finest ! and Skyme at the Lads.

And gallant young Yeomen, our Nation's chief pride,
    For such can be found in no Country beside ;
Each anxiously striving from notice apart,
    To catch a kind look from the Girl of his Heart.

All sports and diversions for old and for Young,
    A medley of frolic is this jovial throng ;
Shrill whistles and trumpets, bag-pipes and gew-gaw
    Pots boiling, Dogs fighting, and game of E. O.

Here's wrestling and vaulting, and dancing on wire,
    With fiddling, and juggling, and men eating Fire,
Bold Serjeants recruiting, Lads 'listing for life,
    And family lessons from Punch and his Wife.

Stalls hung with fine trinkets, before and behind,
    Rich sweets for the palate, and Books for the mind,
Fam'd singers of Ballads, excelled by none,
    And tellers of fortunes, who don't know their own !

Huge giants, dwarf pigmies, wild beasts and wise ponies,
　　Rough bears taught to dance, with arch pug-macaronics !
Raree shows and safe horses, a Penny a ride,
　　With grand entertainments, a thousand beside.

In words all the wonders would never be told,
　　The way to enjoy, is to come and behold ;
The King's Coronation could nothing compare
　　To half the delights of the Magdalen Fair."

The game of " E.O." (v.6.) is the game of badger-baiting.
The badgers were obtained from the woods at Burton
Constable, and were housed in barrels on the Fair ground.
Sometimes there would be a dozen or more present at once.
The man, who wished his dog to try conclusions with the
b adger, paid the owner of the badger sixpence ; but the
attempt to draw the badger not unfrequently ended in the
death of the dog.

CHAPTER III.

Local Customs.

The customs herein mentioned are not exclusively confined to the East Riding of Yorkshire. Their presence here simply means their prevalence in the Riding, as their absence might mean they were unknown as Local Customs.

When a boy goes to school in new clothes, he has to undergo a penalty of pinching from his companions, who say, while he dances under their caresses,

> " Nip for new,
> Two for blew,
> And three for coddiroy."

Woe unto him who had a suit of corduroy, for his mates would insist on his receiving the full " pound of flesh," though frequently the material was too thick for its inmate to feel much of the pinching.

If a boy borrow a knife, to cut an apple, &c., he is told to " send it back laughing :" that is, give a part of the good things to the lender, for the loan of the knife.

Should a boy lose anything, his comrades will join in the

search; but, as, through his carelessness he deserves never to have it again, they say :—

> "Lossin's, seekin's,
> Finndin's, keepin's."

If several boys be together when anything is found, the finder may keep it if he can say " Neeah nowts;" but if the others cry out "shares" before he can speak, he must share the treasure-trove with them.

In playing at marbles, if one boy should "shegger" (win all from) his opponent, it is considered fair and right, nay, mean and shabby not, to give some back, to "set him up," as they call it; such "setting up" being proportionate to the number won. The one who has been "set up" may then challenge his opponent to another game, and his opponent would be bound to accept the challenge, probably causing the winnings to change hands. Should the former loser again lose, he would receive fewer to set him up, and after the third loss would be set up no more.

A like custom obtains among horse and cattle dealers, and similar traders, who always give back to the buyer part of the purchase money, to ensure luck. They can tell instances where the cattle, which had been bought, turned out badly, or even died, when they did not see part of "their own" again. Best, in his *Rural Economy*, (p. 113), says "I have knowne 4 Lambes sold for 11 pence, and the seller gave the buyer a penny again."

Boys, instead of taking their oath, spit their faith, or, spit their death, as it is sometimes called. A third party comes up, and asks "Tom, will tha fight Jack?" "Hey! onny day!" "Jack, will tha fight Tom?" "Hey! noo, if he likes." "Then, best cock spit ower mah lahtle finger." Both do so, and are pledged to fight whenever time and place can be found. Debts of honour are not more binding among men than this act is among boys.

When boys make a raid on an orchard, in spite of Awd Goggie, they put the apples or pears into a "mellow hole" —a hole in the ground, or in a stack. The fruit is then covered up, and left to ripen, or mellow. Housewives used to bury bottled fruits, and if they did not mark the place, which they rarely did, for fear of thieves, the place was sometimes forgotten, and the fruit lost. Buried in this manner, there are twelve bottles of gooseberries somewhere about Scarborough Castle Hill, unless they have been unearthed by some one more fortunate than the good house-wife who buried them.

When farm servants are engaged, or re-engaged, it is customary to give them a sum of money, called a "fest" or "fest-penny." The amount varies from one shilling to one pound, according to the wages of the receiver. A servant is not considered properly engaged unless this "fest" be given and received; and when once received, the agreement is unbreakable save by mutual consent. So the recruiting sergeant gives the Queen's shilling to his recruits. Best, in his *Rural Economy* (p. 133) calls this gift a god's penny :— " Wee have usually two mayd servants, and wee weare wont that wee could hyre them for 18s. per annum, and 12d or 1s. 6d. for a godspenny."

An ancient custom, once observed in the northern parts of the Riding, was "bonnin awd witch" *—(burning the old witch). On the last day of the harvest, a fire of stubble was made in the fields, and peas parched therein. These were eaten with a plentiful allowance of ale, the lads and lasses romping round the fire, and deriving great fun from the blackening of each other's faces.

At Bridlington, on the Sunday night preceding the fair,

* This old witch must not be confounded with the old women called witches. It is really a bad fairy.

which is held on the Monday before Whit Sunday, the boys
used to assemble on the Church Green, where the fair was
held, each armed with a lump of chalk, and each intent on
chalking the backs of as many of the other boys as possible.
This often led to quarrels, as the boys then had on their
Sunday clothes. Notwithstanding this objectionable practice
there was generally a good muster of boys, as preparations
were being made for the coming day.

Farm lads and lasses have a week holiday at Martinmas,
and on Martinmas Sunday a grand dinner is provided for
them at their homes, and to this such ample justice is done
that the day has received a special name—Rive-Kite Sunday
(Tear-Stomach Sunday). A "yat yal posset" (hot ale posset),
ale heated, sweetened with treacle, and spiced, is considered
a proper drink for the day; though many prefer gin, hot
water, and treacle.

When a house, in course of erection, was thatched or
tiled over, it used to be a common custom for all the workmen to have a covering-in-supper, often provided at a public
house. The proprietor of the house gave a donation towards
the expenses, and each of the masters of the various trades
engaged on the work added their donations; generally sufficient to cover the cost, but if not, a collection was made in
the room after the supper, to make up the deficiency. These
suppers often led to an amount of drunkenness, and frequently to the loss of the next day's work, the drinking being
sometimes continued till the early hours of the morning;
but police restrictions have put an end to these all-night
revels. As soon as the roof timbers are in position, the workmen
expect to have an allowance of beer, and then they hoist a
little flag. When a house was being erected for a teetotaller,
he refused to give this offering to Bacchus, so the workmen
bought the driest red herring they could find—one with its
dry mouth wide open, as though it had died of thirst, and

this, with a black streamer, to shew their pitiable condition, was hoisted instead of the "red, white, and blue."

When a cottager killed his pig he used to make a quantity of black-puddings, and invite his friends and neighbours to a black-pudding feast. This was considered the proper thing to do, and none so mean as he who did it not. Though this customary feast is dying out, plates of "pig cheer," containing scraps and cuttings, succulent and savoury, or pork pies, firm as rocks, are still sent to close friends and neighbours.

In concluding a bargain or compact, there need be no word spoken—the two contracting parties simply shake hands, and the agreement is binding;—they have given their hands to it.

When people remove from one house to another, they must invite their friends to a supper. This is called "hoose-warmin" (house warming); but the custom is almost obsolete, except in the case of public-houses.

Raising herrings is a curious custom carried out by the women folk of Flambrough. The old folks hold the opinion that a good fishing season is sure to follow this custom. The young married women dress in various disguises, and, with music and merriment, go about the town, calling at various houses, receiving money or good wishes. The custom is often carried out by those who have been unfortunate at their craft, and the generosity of their neighbours helps to make up the deficiency.

The Curfew Bell is rung every evening at St. Michael's, Spurriergate, York; at Cottingham; and at Hessle, after which is tolled the day of the month. At Driffield, during the harvest month, the church bell is rung every morning at 5 o'clock, and every evening at 7 o'clock, as a signal for the commencement and cessation of labour. It is called the Harvest Bell. This bell is not rung on Sundays; but every Sunday throughout the year a bell is rung at 5 o'clock, an hour before service time, either to drive the evil spirits out of the church, or to give the parishioners ample time for dressing. Perhaps it does both.

Captain E. Anderson, in his auto-biographical poem *The Sailor*, gives the following respecting a custom at Hornsea Marr (Mere) :—

> " Many go there to fish for pleasure sake,
>   But they must always pay for what they take ;
>   When caught, they weigh it at the New Inn door,
>   The money it is given to the poor."

This custom is obsolete, but the Mere is now (1890) open to anglers and boatmen.

The perambulation of boundaries was, in old times, made in the form of a procession, headed by priests bearing crosses; —hence the name Cross Day. Archbishop Grindal, in his *Injunctions to the Clergy of the Diocese of York*, 1571, says : "That the minister use none other ceremonies than to say the 103rd and 104th Psalms, and such sentences of Scripture as be appointed by the Queen's Injunctions, with the Litany and Suffrages following the same, and reading one Homily already decreed and set forth for the purpose ; without wearing any surplice, carrying of banners or hand-bells, or staying at crosses, or such like Popish ceremonies."

Thus the practice was left in the hands of the Church-wardens, Parish Clerk, and minor officials, who, by means of bribing the youngsters to go with them, kept the custom alive until now ; and should the weather be bright and mild on the Rammalation Day, some sprightly octogenarian may be tempted to beat the bounds again for the days of " Auld Lang Syne."

At Beverley, "Rammalation Day" is Rogation Monday. What a day of merriment it is to the boys ! At certain places, money, nuts, and oranges, are scrambled for, and, as ditches form the boundary here and there, great fun is caused by throwing the money and oranges into the water, the youngsters jumping in and splashing about in the water. He who knows the boundary stones will run on ahead ; and, if found sitting there alone, receives a shilling. If two or more are there, the shilling is divided among them. However, more than two rarely stay at one stone, but run on to the next one. When the perambulation is complete, the St. Nicholas party go to the Minster, where they are regaled with beer and buns ; the former served in small mugs. No one is supposed to be served twice, but the young rascals go round the corner, as though going home, change jackets and caps, and return for a second or even third "dollup."

In the parish of All Saints, York, the perambulation of the boundaries was performed on Ascension Day. The lads of the parish got little bundles of sedge, and, while the clerk was inscribing the boundaries at the specified places, they struck his legs below the knee with their wisps. When the clerk wore knee breeches the whipping might be effective. How the boys did strive for a place near to that unfortunate man ! The practice was discontinued about 40 years ago.

At St. Michael's Church, Spurriergate, York, a bell is rung every morning (Sundays excepted), at six o'clock, and afterwards the number of the day of the month. It is related that a traveller once lost his way in the forest which formerly surrounded York, and, after wandering about all night, discovered his whereabouts by hearing the clock of St. Michael's strike six. To commemorate his gratitude, he left a sum of money, so that henceforward the bell might be rung every morning at that time. Another curious custom in connection with this church, was that, on Ascension Day, ale and bread and cheese were given away in the church, to the poor of the parish. The custom has been given up in late years.

To excite public opinion against a wife-beater, it is customary to "ride the stang" for him. A "stee" (ladder) is procured, and a noisy procession perambulates the streets,

singing and shouting, and making night hideous with the braying of horns, clashing of iron pans, screaming of whistles, and banging of drums. This must be done on three successive nights to make it legal, or the "riders" believe they could be summoned for breaking the peace. This custom was observed in Hedon, on the 18th, 19th, and 20th February, 1889, and a correspondent thus describes the route :—
" We started at Church Gate, and went across Market Hill, to Station ; came right up Bedlam Street, through Market Place, and Soutter Gate, to Haven Side ; came back down Fletcher Gate, and Baxter Gate, then George Street, through Market Place again, up to the Market Hill, where we burnt him."

The following doggerel is from *Folk Speech of East Yorkshire* :—

" Here we cum, wiv a ran a dan dan ;
  It's neeather fo' mah cause nor tha cause that Ah ride this stang,
  Bud it is fo' Jack Nelson, that Roman-nooased man.
  Cum all you good people that live i' this raw,
  Ah 'd he' ya tak wahnin, fo' this is oor law ;
  If onny o' you husbans your gud wives do bang,
  Let em cum to uz, an we 'll ride em the stang.
  He beat her, he bang'd her, he bang'd her indeed ;
  He bang'd her afooar she ivver stood need.
  He bang'd her wi' neeather stick, steean, iron, nor stower,
  Bud he up wiv a three-legged stool an knockt her backwards ower.
  　　Up stairs aback o' bed,
  　　Sike a racket there they led.
  　　Doon stairs, aback o' deer,
  　　He buncht her whahl he meead her sweear.
  Noo, if this good man dizzant mend his manners,
  The skin of his hide sal gan ti the tanner's ;
  An if the tanner dizzant tan it well,
  He sal ride upon a gate spell ;
  An if the spell sud happen ti crack,
  He sal ride upon the devil's back ;
  An if the devil sud happen ti run,
  We 'll shut him wiv a wahld-goose gun ;

C

> An if the gun sud happen ti miss fire,
> Ah 'll bid ya good neet, for Ah 's ommast tired."

According to the Constable MSS., the Rector of Easington used to sit on a tombstone, in Easington Churchyard, and there receive of fifty inhabitants the sum of £50 for Easter offerings.

Captain Edward Anderson says :—*

> " In harvest, when it came a windy day,
>   The sheaves and pea-reaps oft were blown away,
>   Mixed, and against some balk or hill were blown ;
>   The farmers then they could not know their own.
>   Some then would take advantage of the rest,
>   At such a time the strongest man fared best.
>   This caused disputes, which they could not prevent,
>   Some suffering loss, were forced to be content.
>   Neighbour 'gainst neighbour had perpetual jars,
>   Town against town were constantly at wars ;
>   He who so rash as for his friend durst plead
>   Was like to get a blow or broken head ;
>   They seldom then did to the lawyer go,
>   Disputes were mostly settled by club-law.
>   Then, after church, upon the Sabbath day,
>   Both old and young would run to football play ;
>   The only prize they could expect to win
>   Was to get broken leg or broken shin."

The following describes the last Race Sunday at Beverley.

It had been the custom, in the days of our grandfathers, to hold a tea-meeting in the Grand Stand, on the Beverley Race Course, on the Sunday before the races, which were held in the spring and summer of each year ; these gatherings being looked forward to with joyful anticipations by the tradespeople and better class inhabitants of the town, who went with their wives and friends, from the neighbouring villages, and had a thorough enjoyable time together.

* *The Sailor*, p. 40.

On these Sundays, it was usual for the young men from the villages around Beverley to assemble in response to a challenge from the lads of that town, to try their manhood in a football contest. At that day there would not be any code of rules, but certain regulations were laid down and strictly adhered to. Rugby was an unknown factor in the calculations of the players. Sterling manhood and swiftness of foot formed the passport they brought with them to the scene of action, and it often stood them in good stead ; for, when the excitement grew high, their physical powers were sorely tried, and the weakest had to retire from the contest. From their elevated position, the occupants of the Grand Stand looked on and applauded the contest as their friends on one side or the other seemed likely to gain the day. The Beverley men were the favourites, and it was only seldom they failed to get the ball into the town, the goal being in North Bar Street, opposite St. Mary's Church. On one of these Sundays the game had been contested more closely than usual, and the villagers had fought the Beverley lads every inch of the way to the town, and Bob Spence, the butcher, had saved their honour by his famous kick from the corner of the Rose and Crown Inn over the North Bar, which kick the old veterans used to boast of over their pipes and ale of an evening, many years after poor Bob was mingled with the dust. The rush through the North Bar had been terrific, and the Mayor (Sammy Hall) who was leaving the church at the time, being near the Bar, was, with his escort of officers, overthrown and trampled on by the crowd, so intent were they on their game. He was quickly raised to his feet, uttering threats of vengeance to those who had subjected him to such rough treatment, and the following year, at the spring races, he tried to carry them out. He, at that time failed, only to return to the attack in the summer, with redoubled vigour and determination. The winter gave place to spring, and the race Sunday came again, and with it the usual game of football. Secretly as the Mayor had devised his plans for its suppression, they leaked out, and plots and counter-plots were the order of the day. The eventful morning dawned at last—one of those sunny April days to be remembered. The sun shone down on the beautiful hill sides, and in the grassy valleys of the pleasant Westwood bright-eyed daises decked the green, and in the shelter of the Pits the fragrant primrose reared its modest head. The rooks were feeding on the high green, and the Pits and Burton-Bushes were vocal with the songsters, which peopled every bush and tree, while the lark, carolling high in the air, looked down on as fair a scene as ever gladdened the heart of man. Yet, though all things in nature were sweet and beautiful, men's passions were only waiting for an opportunity to develope themselves, and transform this happy scene into one of strife and tumult. During the morning, the neighbouring villagers began to arrive in the town, and join the townspeople, who stood in groups at the corners of the streets, and appeared to be discussing the one engrossing topic of the day, and their determination to bring off the football match. As the hour of noon approached, they gradually drew nigh to St. Mary's Church, where the Mayor was at morning service, and when the pealing of the organ announced its close, some spirits, more impetuous than the others, pressed round the door, which was thrown open as the Mayor, with his attendants, could be seen coming down the aisle. As soon as his Worship was clear of the church, he was greeted with a storm of hisses, for which he appeared to be prepared, as it only provoked a sinister smile, boding ill for the success of the sports. After dinner, the townsfolk and their visitors wended their way to the Westwood, and soon the Stand was filled with a gay company, who looked with anxious eyes on the scene below them.

When three o'clock was proclaimed from St. Mary's, the players began to take sides and prepare for action. Bill Hartley, of the Globe Inn, threw the ball into the air, and the game began in the front of the Stand. After a grand struggle, Beverley got the ball clear of the crowd, and headed it towards the town. As it rolled towards the hedge, George Ruddock, the town's bellman, who had lain on the grass, in plain clothes, sprang to his feet, and, seizing it in his arms, made for the hedge, on the other side of which he had a horse waiting for him, held by another constable. He reached the hedge, which was too high to jump, and he began to clamber over it. This was a difficult job, as it was made of strong and prickly thorns, and Nemesis was on his track. Just as he placed his foot on the top, and was preparing to spring over, Bob Pratt, a daring pugilist, caught him by the heel, and held him, till others came up. He was then without mercy dragged face downwards along the top of the hedge, for more than fifty yards, till he was almost disembowelled. He had, at the moment of seizure, thrown the ball to Robert Kemp, one of the town's sergeants, who, running to catch it, slipped and fell on his knees. John Hardman, who had got over the hedge in quest of the ball, hurled a large piece of chalkstone, which, striking the sergeant on his hatless head, bounced off, and sped many yards further, leaving Kemp "hors de combat." The ball was recovered, and the other constables, after an ineffectual struggle, retired from the contest, much discomfited. The game was resumed without further interruption, and was, by the skill of the Beverley men, once more made by the town. So ended this contest, to the great joy of the inhabitants. But baffled men, when they are determined men, are more dangerous than defeated ones. A defeated man accepts the inevitable, but a baffled one seeks for some other, and more successful, mode of securing his

revenge. So it was with the Mayor. He had tried the
civil force, and it had failed. He next had recourse to the
military, and was more successful, as the sequel will show.
Summer once more gladdened the earth, and the usual preparations were made for the Race Sunday, and the football
play. The Westwood was thronged, as usual, with pleasure-
seekers, and the Stand was bright with "fair women and
brave men." The only difference in the beautiful old pasture
was, that the grass had lost its emerald greenness, and had
turned brown under the scorching summer sun. People
seemed to feel that this would be the last Race Sunday, and
assembled in greater numbers than usual, in honour of the
occasion. At the usual hour of three, the ball was thrown
up, and all the famous players were at their posts. An
uneasy feeling pervaded them, as there was no enemy in
view, with whom they could try conclusions, and, knowing
with whom they had to deal, they were satisfied he was
hatching mischief against them, but they could not tell from
what quarter it would come. The usual struggle took place,
and at one time the ball was headed for Walkington, with
every prospect of being got there; but the Beverley lads
made an extra effort, and the ball was once more turned
townwards, when a cry was heard from the Stand which
caused both sides to pause. The cry was "Look out, the
soldiers are coming!" and so it was. Mounted on his
grey horse, sat the Mayor, riding at the head of the
militia, some forty strong. They approached the players
who received them with derisive shouts. The Mayor read
the Riot Act in dumb show, his voice being drowned in
hoarse cries and offensive allusions to his private life. The
game was renewed, but the order was given to the soldiers.
They fixed bayonets, and charged the players, who broke
before them. They then wheeled round and re-charged
them, driving them into little knots, till they were completely

broken up; and, seeing it would be impossible to carry on the game, were compelled to desist. So ended the last game of football on a Race Sunday, and also the last Race Sunday gathering at Beverley.— (An old Freeman of the Borough).

"MY LORD FINCHE'S CUSTOME ATT WATTON FOR CLIPPINGE. *

Hee hath usually fower severall keepinges shorne alltogeather in the Hall-garth, viz.; two from Hawitt; one keepinge from the Court-garth, which is on the west side of South Dalton as wee goe to Weeton; and a fourth from a place adjoining to Huggett field. He hath had 49 clippers all at once, and theire wage is, to each man 12d a day, and, when they have done, beere, bread and cheese; the traylers have 6d a day. His tenants the graingers are tyed to come themselves, and winde the woll, they have a fatte weather and a fatte lamb killed, and a dinner provided for theire paines; there will bee usually three score or fower score poore folkes gatheringe up the lockes, to oversee whome standeth the steward and two or three of his friends or servants with each of them a rodde in his hand; there are two to carry away the woll, and weigh the woll soe soone as it is wounde up, and another that setteth it downe, ever as it is weighed; there is 6d allowed to a piper † for playinge to the clippers all the day; the shepheards have each of them his bell-weathers fleece."

It is customary to provide large rich cheese-cakes, for clipping time, which are known as "clippin chis-keeaks," and it is considered, by the villagers and other friends, quite a treat to obtain a taste of one.

When corn was sent to the mill to be ground, the miller was paid in kind, and retained part of what he ground.

* Best, p 96.

† This is a very late notice of the old English bagpipe, as continuing to exist in Yorkshire.

This was termed "mootherin," and any man who took more
than his due was said to "knaw hoo ti moother." The men
who collected the corn for the millers were termed "cadgers,"
which name is retained in Cadger Lane, leading from the
Little Driffield Road to King's Mill. As these men called
at nearly every house, their horses were constantly stopping
to receive something; hence the saying "As impident as a
cadger hoss."

CHAPTER IV.

Minor Superstitions and Beliefs.

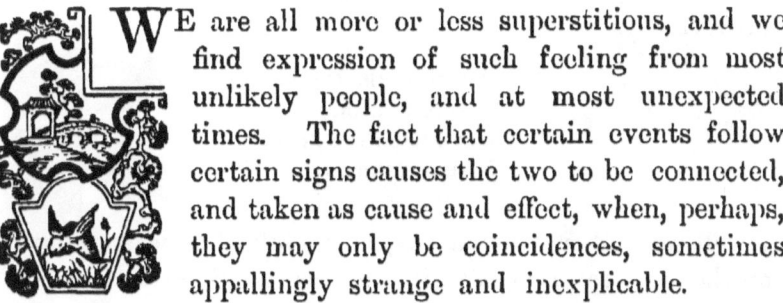

WE are all more or less superstitious, and we find expression of such feeling from most unlikely people, and at most unexpected times. The fact that certain events follow certain signs causes the two to be connected, and taken as cause and effect, when, perhaps, they may only be coincidences, sometimes appallingly strange and inexplicable.

There are two forms of superstition respecting evergreens which have been used for Christmas decorations. One is, that it is wrong, a kind of defiance of the gods, to burn them at all. They ought to be thrown out to decay. As children, we used to delight in seeing the fierce spouting flames which issued from the dried evergreens, though over our joy there hovered a fear of impending direful results. Some say that the evergreens must be removed and burnt before twelfth night. If they remain in position for a longer period something serious will happen. A young lady told me that, in the year 1884, they did not remove the evergreens until February, and in April of the same year her mother had a paralytic stroke, and from that time to this (1889) has never left her bed-room. Cause and effect!

Last summer (1889) a lady of Hull went abroad for the sake of her health, but, becoming worse, died at Boulogne. The old housekeeper, left at home to look after the house, declared that she knew the very hour in which her mistress died, for she heard three distinct taps at the window, the yard-dog howled for no accountable reason, a large mirror in the door of a wardrobe cracked with a loud report, and two pictures on the landing fell, and were broken.

The little white specks, sometimes seen on the nails of the left hand, signify gifts on the thumb; friends on the first finger; foes on the second; lovers on the third; a journey to be undertaken on the fourth. A Holderness proverb says:—

> "A gift on the thumb
> Is sure to come,
> But one on the finger
> Is sure to linger."

I well remember, when a boy, how a school-mate speculated on the appearance of a "gift" on his thumb, as to what the gift would be; for he certainly believed there was one in store for him. How delighted he was when a letter was received, saying his uncle was coming to visit his widowed mother, and bring a watch for him.

Schoolboys believe that if their hands be rubbed with an onion or green walnut shells, or if they wrap a hair round the "bole" of the hand, the schoolmaster's cane, when applied to such a hand so protected, cannot only be not felt but will split the cane from top to bottom. I have seen hands almost black through the use of walnut juice; and during the shelling season, almost every boy carries a piece in his pocket, to be furtively applied, when punishment looms large and near. They will also spit on their hands to avert

evil effects of a stroke, just as they will spit when they meet
a white horse, to avoid the ill consequences of such an
unlucky meeting. After which operation, the following
rhyme is said :—

> " Good luck to you, good luck to me,
> Good luck for every white horse I see."

The first money taken in any undertaking is spit upon for
luck.

Among unlucky things may be mentioned, thirteen sitting
down to dinner ; the crossing of knives on the dinner table ;
to turn back for some forgotten article ; to go under a
ladder ; to enter a house with a tool of any kind over your
shoulder ; to depart from a house leaving "thruf-oppen decars"
(doors open through the house), the back door must be closed
before the front door is opened ; the falling of a picture ; the
cracking of a looking-glass or drinking-glass ; to have a
black cat, though it is lucky to meet one, and unlucky to
meet a coloured one, especially yellow ; to cut the baby's
nails before the child is twelve months old, they must be
bitten off, if need be ; to allow the baby to see itself in a
mirror before it is a year old ; or to spill salt, for every
grain spilt represents a tear you will shed. The offer to help
to salt would be rejected :—

> " Help me to salt,
> Help me to sorrow."

A person who is always in trouble and ill-luck, and so
has become a useless fellow, is known as an "awd knock
saut" (old knock salt). Is it because he has knocked over
or spilled so much metaphoric salt ?

Cinders which fly out of the fire are termed coffins or
purses, according as they are long and narrow, or more or
less circular ; or as they are mute, or emit sounds. If the

cinder gives out a clinking sound it is prophetic of a fortune; if noiseless it foretells a funeral.

To dream of your teeth falling out is a bad sign, foretelling some fearful unknown thing. To get out of bed with the left foot first renders you cross and unfortunate all the day. A boy, who had been cross and contrary all day, was told by his mother to go to bed again, for he had "gotten oot o' bed wrang foot fost."

When your right ear tingles, some one is speaking well of you; if the left, evil speaking against you is being indulged in; while, if you shiver, some one is walking over your grave. Should your nose itch, you will soon be angry; if the right eye, a surprise awaits you; if the left, you will soon cry; if the right foot, a journey is before you. Itching of the palm of the right hand indicates the reception of money by the itching palm; of the left hand, the payment of money by you to others.

When the tallow on the candle forms something like an icicle or stalactite, it is termed a winding-sheet, and is taken as a sign of death. The same is believed if the corpse is "leeath-wake" (does not become rigid about the usual time). If a dead body be carried across a field, that field will become barren, no matter how fruitful previously.

The bright spark in the flame of a candle is called a "letter," and is supposed to betoken a coming letter containing good news; the number of knocks on the table, which it requires to make it fall, being the number of days which will elapse before its arrival.

It is considered very unlucky to give a light to any one on Christmas Day, so that, in olden times, one of the last questions, before going to bed on Christmas Eve, was, "Is the tinder dry, and are the matches well dipped?" My father relates that, when a boy, not having any dry tinder, he could not get a light to make the fire one Christmas morning. He went to get one from an aged woman who lived near; but never a light would she allow to go out of her house, and render herself unlucky. After considerable earnest entreaty she gave her own tinder box, whereby a light could be obtained.

The Northern Lights *(Aurora Borealis)* are supposed to be a sign of war and conflagration. The winter of 1870 was remarkable for the splendid displays of crimson and orange streamers, which were looked upon as the reflection of the immense destruction caused by the Franco-German war.

When the new moon has her horns upward, she is said to be "on her back," and it is commonly believed to betoken fine weather. A sudden period of very fine weather, if unseasonable, is looked upon with distrust, as being too good to last long; and is known as a "weather-breeder," *i.e.*, a forerunner of bad weather.

The loose bits of skin about the finger nails, are known as "idle-backs," and are said to be only on the fingers of those who do no work.

If two persons wash their hands in the same water, they will disagree before bed-time, unless the water be "crossed," by making the sign of the cross with the forefinger.

To stumble when going upstairs is sure sign of a wedding; though to dream of a wedding betokens death.

Persons, whose eyebrows meet, are deemed specially fortunate, as being "lucky" in all their undertakings. A crooked sixpence, or a coin with a hole through it, is sought after, because of the power to confer the much-coveted "luck."

Belemnites are called "thunder-bolts," and are believed to have fallen from the clouds.

If you bite your tongue, while eating your food, it is because you have told a falsehood; and if your new boots creak, the shoemaker is still un-paid.

To wash your hands in water in which eggs have been boiled is a sure way to have warts ; and if a wart bleeds, it is believed that wherever the blood goes there will be more warts. A similar belief exists about corns. If you cut a corn and it bleeds, you will bleed to death. These two latter beliefs have doubtless arisen from witticisms, for neither the wart nor the corn can bleed, and are on a par with the saying by which children are mystified, when such and such a statue *hears* twelve o'clock strike he will descend from his pedestal to get his dinner.

On our coast, if fishermen meet a woman with a white apron, when they are going to sea, they will turn back and wait a tide. In folk lore, the feminine sex carry ill-luck with them, whether as "first foot," or in the shape of a cat, a hare (which is always spoken of as feminine), or a horse.

My father, when travelling on foot, noticed a good nail laid on the road, and, thinking it would be useful at some house where he intended calling, picked it up and carried it to the nearest house. The old dame held up her hands in dismay, as it was offered to her, and said "Ah hardly knaw what ti say ti ya! Yu meean weel, bud thraw it oot at decar. Ah can't bide ti see it." "But it's a good nail, and you may want one." "Nivver mind! Thraw it away!" and her evident terror was not allayed until the unlucky thing had been taken out of the house, because it is reckoned most unlucky to bring old iron into a house.

You run the risk of losing your sweetheart, if you have one, by putting cream in your tea before sugar ; or, at least, you will cross your love, if you do not sever it. No young man will think of presenting his friend or sweetheart with knife, scissors, or any sharp-edged tool ; it would cut their friendship or love. But if a small coin or other article be given in exchange, no evil result will follow. The following lines, bearing on this subject, are not without interest. They were written by the Rev. Samuel Bishop, in 1796, when presenting his wife with a knife, on their fifteenth wedding-day :—

> " A knife, dear girl, cuts love they say,
>   Mere modish love perhaps it may ;
>   For any tool of any kind
>   Can separate what was never joined.
>   The knife that cuts our love in two
>   Will have much tougher work to do,—
>   Must cut your softness, worth and spirit,
>   Down to the vulgar size of merit ;
>   To level yours with common taste
>   Must cut a world of sense to waste ;
>   And from your single beauty's store
>   Chip what would dizen out a score.
>   The self same blade from me must sever
>   Sensation, judgment, sight for ever !
>   All memory of endearments past,
>   All hope of comforts long to last,
>   All that makes fourteen years with you
>   A summer, and a short one too.
>   All that affection feels and fears,
>   When hours without you seem like years.
>   Till that be done – and I'd as soon
>   Believe this knife would clip the moon—
>   Accept my present undeterred
>   And leave their proverbs to the herd.
>   If in a kiss—delicious treat—
>   Your lips acknowledge their receipt,
>   Love, fond of such substantial fare,
>   And proud to play the glutton there,
>   All thoughts of cutting will disdain,
>   Save only—' cut and come again.' "
>   (Henderson, p. 118)

Unless a shearer cuts himself with the sickle the first time he uses it, he will never be expert with that implement.

(Best, p. 43).

Mishaps follow each other in threes. A boy who cuts his hand expects to do so other twice. A breakage of crockery is sure to be followed by two more, and the anxious house-wife hails the third breakage with a sigh of relief, as bringing a respite, for a time at least, from further destruction.

When any fruit having stones, such as cherry, plum, &c., is eaten, the stones are used in peeping into the future with respect to marriage, the following formula being used :—

> This year,
> Next year,
> Sometime,
> Never,

one stone for each line, and the time, which falls to the last stone, is the destined time.

D

OWTHORNE CHURCH.

[About 1800.]

CHAPTER V

𝔓lace 𝔏egends and 𝔗raditions.

"I cannot tell how the truth may be;
I say the tale as 'twas said to me."

The Lay of the Last Minstrel, c. ii. 8, 22.

THE manors of Owthorne and Withernsea, so says tradition, once belonged to two sisters, who determined on building a church for their tenantry and dependents; and as the two manors were adjoining it was thought one church would be sufficient for both. The site of Owthorne church was accordingly fixed upon, and the building rose to a certain height when the sisters differed as to whether it should have a tower or a spire. To settle matters one was built by each lady on her own ground, and to her own taste. These were known as the "Sister Kirks;" but that of Owthorne was undermined, and finally washed away by the sea about 1824. One of the tombstones from this churchyard, unearthed after a storm, was used by a farmer as a hearthstone, with the lettering downwards. After some years a succeeding tenant took up this hearthstone to make place for another, and was surprised, on turning it over, to find that it was a record of death. Not liking to destroy it, he put it in the barn to take care of it, and thought no more about it, until one day a stranger from America came into the village making enquiries about his ancestors, in order to complete his pedigree. No one could give him the information he sought, for his fore-elders had left the place long years before, until it was remembered that a name, like the one he sought, was on this nearly-forgotten tombstone. It was eagerly brought to light again, and supplied him with the very information he had travelled thousands of miles to obtain.

Previous to a storm, as the sea comes "suthering" (sobbing and sighing) up to the beach, there comes also another sound, the mournful dirge of the ghostly choir, who still chant their low-voiced psalms from their usual seats in the engulfed channel; and anon may be heard the slow tolling of the bells, calling the hearer to join in their service.

It is said the bells of Owthorne church were re-cast and formed into the bells of Driffield Linseed Cake Mill, bells noted for their clear silvery tone. When the mill was destroyed by fire in 1887, the fierce heat melted the bells, but the greater part was secured by Messrs. Shipham, brass founders, Hull, who made it into small articles, ash-trays, tobacco jars, table bells, &c., as mementos for their friends.

The peculiar mournful sighing of the sea is sometimes called "Aubro Dol," and there is a tradition that the bells of the destroyed church of Aldborough can still be heard ringing beneath the waves.

Under the chancel of Hornsea church there is a vaulted crypt, known as Awd Nanny Canker Hole, the old entrance to which was under the east window, but is now walled up and a fresh entrance made. This crypt used to be a place for the concealment of smuggled goods. On the night of the 23rd of December, 1732, the parish clerk was concealing goods here when a sudden hurricane unroofed the church, and blew down the steeple, which has never been re-erected. A windmill was overturned by the violence of the storm, and the millstones carried 150 yards away. Sheets of lead were blown from the church and wrapped round two sycamore trees in Hall Garth. A woman and child in bed together had their house unroofed, and the bed with them in it was blown into the street and neither of them injured; a wooden beam from the roof of one house was blown across the street into a garret window opposite.

Who does not know the Flambro' caves, and who has not heard of the legend connected with Robin Lythe Hole, that wonderful cave with its sea and land entrances, its lofty irregular roof, its bright slippery floor, its fine effects of light and shade, the cathedral-like aspect of the farther end with its white steps and marble-like altar? and who has not looked at the shelf of rock across the cavern from side to side, just within the seaward entrance and wondered how anyone could find a place of safety there, as Robin Lythe did when his vessel was wrecked and he was washed ashore into this very cavern? Another cavern, the Kirk Hole, is said to extend from the north shore, underground and inland, to the church a considerable distance away.

One of the numerous Gipsey springs which burst out at the foot of the Wolds, after a wet autumn, leaps out of the Henpit Hole, near Killam, with such force that a man on horseback can ride under the arch thus formed without getting wet. It takes its name from the tradition that a hen once came out there having been carried underground from Langtoft well.

At West Field, Killam, there is a hollow, probably a disused chalk-pit, bearing the name of Peg Fyfe Hole, because it was used by Peg Fyfe and her band as a hiding place. As nearly every pit and hollow is haunted, and consequently held in dread, such a place was probably secure.

Near Holme-on-Spalding-Moor is a small moated building bearing the name Monk Farm. According to tradition, a cell for two monks was established here, either by one of the Vavasours of Spaldington or the Constables of Holme, and it was the duty of one of them to guide travellers over this swampy moor, while the other was imploring the protection of heaven for those exposed to the dangers of the road. These offices they performed alternately.

Lind House, near Hunmanby, is so called because of a visit paid to it by the celebrated songstress, Jenny Lind, on the 14th September, 1848, while staying at Filey. It is said that it was Miss Lind's intention to visit Field House, that being the largest farm, but the occupiers of both farms having the name of Simpson, her conductor took her in mistake to Graffitoe House, which thus had "greatness thrust upon it."

Mount Spaniel, near Kilham, is so named because one of its occupiers, Arthur Ness, kept several spaniels, which informed him of the approach of visitors, desirable and otherwise. As a result of proceedings at law, he had to be served with a writ, but all attempts to serve it failed, for the dogs gave him warning when anyone came, and if they looked writ-like, he was not to be found. A local constable at last undertook the task, and disguised himself as a pig-jobber, for his intended prey had two weaknesses, spaniels and pigs. The bait took, and more business was transacted that day than was agreeable to Arthur Ness. The writ was a command to sign a certain document, which he refused to do, and for contempt of court was committed to prison. Nothing daunted, he walked all the way to London, and the person in whose favour the document would have been had to keep him while there.

About a mile and a half from Beverley Minster, near Killingwoldgraves, in a field by the road-side, is a broken pillar, called Stump Cross. It is about five feet high, and bears an almost effaced inscription, which was deciphered in 1773, as follows :—

Orate Pro Anima Magistri Willielmi de Walthon.

(Pray for the soul of Master William of Walthon).

This has led to the belief that the cross was erected to commemorate a murder committed here ; but it is doubtless one of the Beverley Sanctuary crosses, with the inscription added at a later date, and totally unconnected with the purpose of the original cross.

Opposite a break in the immense earthworks at Skipsea Brough are four footprints in the grass field. Here, it is said, two brothers fought a duel, and the place where their feet were is accursed, and has never grown grass since. The footprints are two or three inches deep, are plainly " rights " and " lefts " and at fighting distance apart. At Hutton Cranswick, there are also two footprints, but barren from a very different cause to those at Skipsea Brough. A fine fellow was Tommy Escritt, one of nature's noblemen, who, though but a humble farm servant, was beloved alike by rich and poor, for genuine sterling worth. A fervent Methodist he, and powerful preacher too, and as he ascended the hill to his daily work at Burn Butts, he used to stand for a few minutes overlooking the village of Cranswick, and pray for its conversion. There to this day are the marks of his feet, for no grass grows on this place, so sacred to his memory ; a place to which visits and pilgrimages are made, as to some dear spot or holy place.

Before the days of the policeman, one part of the Bayle Gate, Bridlington, was used as a lock-up, and was and is still known as the Kitcote. Here drunkards were imprisoned over-night, to be brought before the magistrates next morning. While in the Kitcote, their mates contrived to supply them with liquor, through the bars of the grating across the square hole in the door of the prison. " Ah can dhrink yal as weel here as onny wheear else, only let's hev it" said the inmates, as the man in the stocks said; so that often the prisoner was more drunk in the morning than when he was imprisoned. In consequence, a perforated iron plate was nailed over the bars, but this only called forth further ingenuity, for the long stem of a "churchwarden" pipe was thrust through one of the holes, and beer poured into the bowl, while the prisoner sucked away contentedly at the other end.

In a hollow on Beverley Westwood is a stone trough, into which a spring of exceedingly cold pure water once flowed abundantly. It is quite dry now, and has been for some years, but it still retains the name of Cobbler Well. Tradition tells how a cobbler of Beverley, jealous of his wife, drowned her in this well, while in a mad drunken state, but he cheated the law by dying almost immediately of remorse and grief.

The following is taken from a newspaper article entitled "Beneath the Snow," by Wm. Andrews, F.R.H.S., to whom Mr. Jno. Browne, of Bridlington, contributed the particulars. "Sarah West, daughter of George West, of Market Weighton, was servant to Mr. Freeman, of Newbald Wold. On Sunday, the 7th of March, 1858, she walked home to see her parents. About four o'clock in the afternoon, she left Market Weighton to return to the Wold, but was overtaken by a severe snowstorm; the flakes falling so thick and fast that she could not see her way. However, she struggled bravely on, but was so fatigued, that, when she fell into a snow-drift, she was unable to rise again. Her struggles only buried her deeper, and as her strength failed she was filled with despair; and the storm continuing, she was soon completely covered. Here she remained until the following Tuesday morning, when the shepherd, passing that way, observed a bonnet lying on the snow. This excited his curiosity, and his search resulted in the discovery of his unfortunate fellow-servant. Help was obtained, and she was speedily conveyed to the farm-house; but she was very weak for lack of food, and her feet were so swollen that her boots had to be cut off. However, by careful nursing, she recovered, and seemed little the worse for her adventure."

The Abbey of Meaux, Holderness, of which there are now scarcely any remains, is said to be connected with Beverley Minster by a subterranean passage. Once, when the monks of the Abbey suffered much for want of food during a siege, a lady of Burstwick volunteered to get supplies from Beverley by means of this passage. For three days she walked from the Minster to the Abbey, laden with provisions, until she died in the passage of exhaustion and fatigue, and her body was not recovered by the monks until some days after.

In Welton Dale there is an old twisted thorn tree, which goes by the name of Tinkler's Bush. The tree is separate from all others, and firmly fixed among its twisted roots and branches are some large stones. These are the very stones which caused the death of poor Deborah Tinkler, the wife of Gideon Tinkler, who was believed to have bewitched her husband, and here suffered the dreadful penalty of being stoned to death.

Part of the Roman encampment at Swine is known as the Giant's Grave. The mound, covered with ash trees is not far from the lines of the Hull and Hornsea Railway.

On the outside wall of St. Mary's Church, Beverley, hangs an oval tablet, bearing the following inscription:—

"Here two young Danish Souldiers lye,
The one in Quarrell chanc'd to dye;
The other's Head by their own Law,
With Sword was sever'd at one Blow.
December the 23d,
1689."

These soldiers had come to join the service of the Prince of Orange, and, while billeted in Beverley, quarrelled about one of the maids at the hostelry. In the fight, or duel, one of

them fell, and the survivor was sentenced by court-martial
to be beheaded for the murder of his comrade. The scaffold
was erected on the Cornhill, in the Market Place, where the
great gas lamp now stands. Two cartloads of gravel had been
fetched from Brandesburton and laid under the scaffold, to
absorb the blood which fell; soldiers were there as a guard,
and crowds of spectators looked on the unusual scene in
silence, and so the law was satisfied, and St. Mary's registers
record the following :—

1689, December 16.—Daniel Straker, a Danish trooper, buried.

,,   December 23.—Johannes Frederick Bellow, a Danish trooper,
                 beheaded for killing the other, buried.

Thompson's *Historical Sketches of Bridlington* contains
the following entry respecting Bridlington Market:—"An
attempt was made by the lord of the manor, in 1788, to
determine the hours of attendance in this market, appointing
the sale of butter, eggs, and poultry, to begin not earlier than
ten o'clock in the morning; nor that of corn before twelve;
and the whole to conclude at three in the afternoon." The
better to enforce these salutary regulations a bell was affixed
to the Pillory, which stood opposite the Corn Exchange, and
this bell was rung at the appointed hours. The regulations
fell into disuse, and as the bell was rung at all hours by the
boys, it was taken down in 1810, and kept in a house down
a court known as Pillory Bell Yard. The Pillory itself stood
until 1835, and lay a long time in Well Lane, forgotten and
uncared for, and then it disappeared, having probably served
as firewood.

In Beverley Minster is a beautiful monument, without
name or date, but it is known as the Sisters' Shrine. The
legend tells of two sisters, maidens, who were nuns at
Beverley. One night they were missed, and could not be
found, though diligent search was made for them. Months
after, they were discovered in a trance in the north tower;

and, on being awakened, told of wonderful sights and sounds
they had seen and heard, while in the heavenly country.

At night, they came to the Abbess and asked her blessing,
for they had been summoned to their long home, and, as
she uttered the words of peace, their gentle spirits fled. The
following verses, bearing on this subject, were first published
in the *Literary Gazette*, anonymously, but have been attributed to Alaric A. Watts.

" The tapers are blazing, the mass is sung
    In the chapel of Beverley,
And merrily too the bells have rung;
    'Tis the eve of our Lord's nativity;
And the holy maids are kneeling round,
While the moon shines bright on the hallowed ground.

Yes, the sky is clear, and the stars are bright,
    And the air is hush'd and mild,
Befitting well the holy night,
    When o'er Judæa's mountains wild,
The mystic star blazed bright and free,
And sweet rang the heavenly minstrelsy.

The nuns have risen; through the cloister dim,
    Each seeks her lonely cell,
To pray alone till the joyful hymn,
    On the midnight breeze shall swell;
And all are gone, save two sisters fair,
Who stand in the moonlight silent there.

Now hand in hand, through the shadowy aisle,
    Like airy things they've passed;
With noiseless step, and with gentle smile,
    And meek eyes heavenward cast;
Like things too pure upon earth to stay,
They have fled like a vision of light away.

And again the merry bells have rung,
   So sweet through the starry sky,
For the midnight mass hath this night been sung,
   And the chalice is lifted high,
And the nuns are kneeling in holiest pray'r;
Yes, all, save these meek-eyed sisters fair.

Then up rose the abbess, she sought around,
   But in vain, for these gentle maids;
They were ever the first at the mass-bell's sound,
   Have they fled these holy shades?
Or can they be numbered among the dead;
Oh! whither can these fair maids be fled?

The snows have fled, the fields are green,
   The cuckoo singeth aloud,
The flowers are budding, the sunny sheen
   Beams bright through the parted cloud,
And maidens are gathering the sweet breath'd May;
But these gentle sisters, oh! where are they?

And summer is come in rosy pride,
   'Tis the eve of the blessed Saint John,
And the Holy nuns after vespertide,
   All forth from the chapel are gone;
While to taste the cool of the evening hour,
The abbess hath sought the topmost tower.

' Gramercy! sweet ladye! and can it be?'
   The long lost sisters fair
On the threshold lie calm, and silently,
   As in holiest slumber there!
Yet sleep they not, but entranced they lie
With lifted hands, and heavenward eye.

' Oh! long lost maidens, arise! arise!
   Say when did ye hither stray?'
They have turned to the abbess with their meek blue eyes?
   ' Not an hour hath passed away
But glorious visions our eyes have seen;
Oh! sure in the kingdom of heaven we've been.'

There is joy in the convent of Beverley
  Now these saintly maidens are found,
And to hear their story right wonderingly
  The nuns have gathered around ;
The long lost maidens, to whom was given
To live so long the life of heaven.

And again the chapel bell is rung,
  And all to the altar repair,
And sweetly the midnight songs are sung,
  By the sainted sisters there.
While their heaven-taught voices softly rise
Like an incense cloud to the silent skies.

The maidens have risen ; with noiseless tread
  They glide o'er the marble floor ;
They seek the abbess with bended head :—
  'Thy blessing we would implore,
Dear mother! for, ere the coming day
Shall burst into light, we must hence away.'

The abbess hath lifted her gentle hands,
  And the words of peace hath said,
'O vade in pacem,' aghast she stands,
  ' Have their innocent spirits fled ?'
Yes, side by side lie these maidens fair,
Like two wreaths of snow in the moonlight there.

List! List! the sweet peal of the convent bells,
  They are rung by no earthly hand,
And hark how far off the melody swells
  Of the joyful angel band,
Who hover around, surpassingly bright,
And the chapel is bathed in rosy light.

'Tis o'er! side by side, in the chapel fair,
  Are the sainted maidens laid ;
With their snowy brow, and their glossy hair.
  They look not like the dead!
Fifty summers have come and passed away
But their loveliness knoweth no decay !

And many a chaplet of flowers is hung,
  And many a bead told there.
And many a hymn of praise is sung,
  And many a lowbreathed prayer;
And many a pilgrim bends the knee,
At the shrine of the Sisters of Beverley."

Near Rudston church stands a well-known monolith, which, tradition says, the devil threw to destroy church and builders. Fortunately, he missed his aim, but there the missile stands, a monument of miscarried malignity.

A middle-age tradition tells us that in one of the violent storms that visited Filey Bay, a hen-coop was washed on shore, and the natives, not understanding what it was, sent for the priest, a drunken old fellow, who, on coming, bade them turn it over. They did so, and he bade them turn it over again, which they did; and then he said he could not tell what it was, but he thought it would make a good organ for the church, and accordingly it was carried there.

The dangerous ridge of rocks known as Filey Brig was built by the devil, who, in building lost his hammer. Plunging into the sea after it, he grasped a fish in his sooty fingers, and exclaimed "Ah! Dick!" The fish has been named *haddock* ever since, and still retains the mark of the satanic grasp across its shoulders.*

On Hornsea gibbet there last hung the body of a notorious smuggler named Pennel, who murdered his captain, and sank the vessel near Hornsea, where he and his companions in crime landed. Through quarrelling, while drunk, their crime was discovered, and they were arrested. Pennel was tried at York, found guilty, and sentenced to be hanged on Hornsea Gibbet. Here his body hung in chains, fully dressed, even to the buckles on his shoes, until someone, more venturesome than the rest, stole the buckles and the best part of the clothing.

* See Appendix A.

FROM A PHOTOGRAPH]　　RUDSTON CHURCH AND MONOLITH.　　[BY W. FISHER, FILEY.

On Cliff Lane, Bempton, are seven or eight large whinstone boulders, and the old people say the stones were washed up over the cliff by the sea. At one time they were scattered about the fields, but were placed in their present position, by the road-side, so as to be "out of the way," and not to interfere with the cultivation of the fields.

At Harpham, there is a well, dedicated to St. John of Beverley, who is said to have been born in this village, and to have wrought many miracles through the virtue of the waters of this well. It is still believed to possess the power of subduing the largest and fiercest animals. William of Malmesbury relates that in his time the most rabid bull, when brought to its waters, became quiet as the gentlest lamb. At the same village there is, in a field near the church, another well, called the Drummer's Well, to which appertains the following story, for which the writer is indebted to Parkinson's *Yorkshire Legends*. "About the time of the second or third Edward—when all the young men of the country were required to be practised in the use of the bow, and for that purpose public 'butts' were found connected with almost every village, and occasionally 'field-days' for the display of archery were held, attended by gentry and peasant alike—the old manor house near this well at Harpham was the residence of the family of St. Quintin. In the village lived a widow, reputed to be somewhat 'uncanny' named Molly Hewson. She had an only son, Tom Hewson, who had been taken into the family at the manor, and the squire, struck with his soldierly qualities, had appointed him trainer and drummer to the village band of archers. A grand field day of these took place in the well-field in front of the manor house. A large company was assembled, and the sports were at their height, the squire and his lady looking on with the rest. But one young rustic proving more than usually stupid in the use of his bow, the squire made a rush forward to chastise him. Tom, the

E

drummer, happened to be standing in his way, and near the
well.   St. Quintin accidentally ran against him and sent
him staggering backward, and tripping, he fell head foremost
down the well.   Some time elapsed before he could be
extricated, and when this was effected the youth was dead.
The news spread quickly, and soon his mother appeared upon
the scene.   At first she was frantic, casting herself upon his
body, and could not realize—though she had been warned of
the danger of this spot to her son—that he was dead. Suddenly
she rose up and stood with upright mien, outstretched arm,
and stern composure, before the squire. She remained silent
awhile, glaring upon him with dilated eyes, while the awe-
stricken bystanders gazed upon her as if she were some
supernatural being.   At length she broke silence, and
exclaimed 'Squire St. Quintin, you were the friend of my
boy, but from your hand his death has come.   Therefore,
whenever a St. Quintin, Lord of Harpham, dies, my poor boy
shall beat his drum at the bottom of this fatal well.'   From
that time, so long as the race lasted, on the eve preceding
the death of the head of the house, the rat-tat of Tom's drum
was heard in the well, by those who listened for it."   It is
the current belief that the bloody hand on the St. Quintin's
Baronet's shield is added because of this unintentional
murder.

St. Austin's stone is a block of natural concrete, standing
at the head of Drewton Dale, near South Cave. It is said
to derive its name from St. Augustine, who used to preach
from this stone to the heathen, before Britain became
Christian.

Near Keyingham is a spring of water called St. Philip's
Well, into which the girls used to drop pins and money when
wishing a wish.

A correspondent writes, concerning Burton Agnes Hall :—
"Some forty years ago, John Bilton, a cousin of mine, came
from London on a visit into the neighbourhood, and having

a relative, Matthew Potter—who was a gamekeeper on the estate—he paid him a visit, and was invited to pass the night there. Potter, however, told him that, according to popular report, the house was haunted, and that if he were afraid of ghosts he had better sleep elsewhere; but John, who was a dare-devil sort of a fellow, altogether untinctured by superstitious fancies, replied, 'Afraid! not I, indeed; I care not how many ghosts there may be in the house so long as they do not molest me.' Potter then told him of the skull and the portrait of 'Awd Nance' and asked him if he would like to see the latter; the skull, it would appear, from what followed, was not then in the house. He replied that he should like to see the picture, and they passed into the room where it was hanging, and Potter held up the candle before the portrait, when, in a moment, and without any apparent cause, the candle became extinguished, and defied all attempts at 'blowing it in again' so they were obliged to grope their way to the bedroom in the dark. They occupied the same bed, and Potter was soon asleep and snoring, but Bilton, ruminating over the tale of the skull and the curious circumstance of the sudden extinction of the light in front of the portrait of the ghost, lay awake. When he had lain musing for half-an-hour, he heard the shuffling of feet outside the chamber door, which at first he ascribed to the servants going to bed, but as the sounds did not cease, but kept increasing, he nudged his bed-fellow, and said 'Matty, what the deuce is all that noise about!' 'Jinny Yewlats' (owls), replied his companion, in a half waking tone, and turning over, again began to snore. The noise became more uproarious, and it seemed as if ten or a dozen persons were scuffling about in the passage just outside, and rushing in and out of the rooms, slamming the doors with great violence, upon which he gave his friend another vigorous nudge in the ribs, exclaiming 'Wake up, Matty; don't you hear that confounded row? What does it all mean?' 'Jinny

Yewlats' again muttered his bed-fellow. 'Jinny Yewlats,' replied Bilton, 'Jinny Yewlats can't make such an infernal uproar as that.' Matty, who was now more awakened, listened and said "'Tis Awd Nance, but Ah nivver take any notice of her,' and he rolled over and again began to snore. After this 'the fun grew fast and furious,' a struggling fight seemed to be going on outside, and the clapping of the doors reverberated in the passage like thunder claps. He expected every moment to see the chamber door fly open, and Awd Nance with a troop of ghosts come rushing in, but no such catastrophe occurred, and after a while the noises ceased, and about daylight he fell asleep." The writer adds, that his cousin, though a fear-naught, and a thorough dis-believer in the supernatural, told him that he never passed so fearful a night before in his life, and would not sleep another night in the place, if he were offered the Hall for doing so. He further adds that his cousin was a thoroughly truthful man, who might be implicitly believed, and that he had this narrative from his own lips on the following day.

The skull, whose displacement causes so much trouble, is believed to belong to one of the reputed builders of the mansion.   All is quiet and peaceable so long as the skull is left alone on its table.   There is a similar tradition respecting the Manor House, at Lund, where the skull has been walled up in the attic to prevent its removal.

CHAPTER VI.

Goblindom.

GHOSTS—APPARITIONS—FAIRIES.

OLD beliefs die hard, so that education and the advancement of knowledge have not yet banished all ghosts and goblins from the earth. Certain old people can yet "see" things, for such sight is not given to every one, the seventh child of a seventh child has wonderful powers of sight over the commonly unseen world.

The appearance of the wraith, or likeness of the departing one, is placed on record in the *Heimskringla*, and is beautifully translated by the poet Longfellow in *Tales of a Wayside Inn*. Odin, in his usual disguise as a one-eyed man, appears at a banquet, which Olaf, the introducer of Christianity into Norway, had prepared. They retired late, and in the morning, the stranger had departed.

> " They found the doors securely barred,
> They found the watch-dog in the yard,
> There was no footprint in the grass,
> And none had seen the stranger pass.
> King Olaf crossed himself and said,
> ' I know that Odin the Great is dead;
> ' Sure is the triumph of our Faith,
> ' The one-eyed stranger was his wraith.' "

The following can be vouched for by persons now living. An old lady in Hull had a son, who was a sailor, and of whose ship they had heard nothing for a long time. One night, as she lay in bed, with the curtains closely drawn round the large four-posted bedstead, she saw, by the dim night light, the curtains noiselessly drawn aside, and the head of her absent son appeared in the opening. The vision soon passed away, leaving a firm conviction that she should never see her son alive again. Her worst fears were confirmed by news brought by another ship, which had found the bodies of the crew of the ill-fated vessel in which her son had sailed.

Captain E. Anderson, in his autobiographical poem *The Sailor,* thus describes his mother's appearance to him at the time of her death :—

> " One of her sons, though in another clime,
> He thought he saw her at the very time.
> He offered her a kiss—she never spoke,
> But smiled on him—then vanished. He awoke.
> Though much astonished, yet he felt no dread,
> But from that time he fancied she was dead.
> He told his shipmates, but they laughed at him,
> And said ' 'Twas but a dream, an idle whim ';
> But when a letter came and it proved true,
> His shipmates then were much astonished too."

Similar instances might be multiplied to almost any extent, but a curious apparition used to be seen in the daytime in the east window of Holy Trinity Church, Micklegate, York. When the church was enlarged about two years ago, the window at which it appeared was taken away, and so it remains an unsolved problem, strange and perplexing. Though never seen now, the old sexton, who has seen it, believes in its presence ; for when he finds any windows open which he thought he had shut, he says the Trinity Ghost has

done it. The following account is taken from Rev. S. Baring
Gould's *Yorkshire Oddities*—"The figures began to move
across the window long before the commencement of the
service, when in fact there was no one present but ourselves.
They did so again before the service began, as well as during
the 'Venite,' and subsequently as many as twenty or thirty
times I should suppose, till the conclusion of the sermon. Of
the three figures, two were evidently those of women, and
the third was a little child. The two women were very
distinct in appearance. One was tall and very graceful, and
the other middle-sized; we called the second one the nurse-
maid from her evident care of the child during the absence
of the mother, which relationship we attributed to the tall
one, from the passionate affection she exhibited towards the
child, her caressing it, and the wringing of her hands over
it. I may add that each figure is perfectly distinct from the
others, and after they had been seen once or twice, are at once
recognisable. The order of their proceedings with slight
variation was this :—The mother came alone from the north
side of the window, and having gone about half-way across,
stopped, turned round, and waved her arm towards the
quarter whence she had come. This signal was answered by
the entry of the nurse with the child. Both figures then
bent over the child and seemed to bemoan its fate; but the
taller one was always the most endearing in her gestures.
The mother then moved towards the other side of the window
taking the child with her, leaving the nurse in the centre of
the window, from which she gradually retired towards the north
corner, whence she had come, waving her hand as though
making signs of farewell as she retreated. After some little
time she again appeared, bending forward and evidently
anticipating the return of the other two, who never failed to
re-appear from the south side of the window where they had
disappeared. The same gestures of despair and distress were
repeated, and then all three retired together to the north

side of the window. Usually they appeared during the
musical portions of the service, and especially during one
long eight-lined hymn, when—for the only occasion without
the child—the two women rushed on (in stage phrase), and
remained during the whole hymn, making the most frantic
gestures of despair. Indeed the louder the music in that
hymn the more carried away with their grief did they seem
to be. Nothing could be more emphatic than the individuality
of the several figures; the manner of each had its own
peculiarity. Where the stained glass was thickest there
the less distinct were the forms. It was like catching
glimpses of them through leaves. But nearer the edge
of the window, where the colours were less bright, they
were perfectly distinct; and still more so on the pane of
unstained glass at the edge. There they seemed most clear,
and gave one the impression of being real persons, not
shadows."

Respecting this apparition another correspondent writes :—
"On Good Friday last I went to Holy Trinity Church,
York, for service at 11 o'clock, and repaired with a friend to
the gallery, being anxious to see an apparition which is said
to haunt the place. The gallery is situated at the extreme
west end of the building, and faces the east window, from
which it is distant some 50 feet or so. It is said that in the
aisle of the body of the church nothing is ever seen. The
gallery was full, but no one seemed to have come there
especially for the ghost, and though many of them afterwards
said they saw it, they were not in the least affected by the
apparition, treating it as a matter of course, to which they
were all accustomed. I kept my eyes fixed on the east
window, for nearly the whole of the hour and a half during
which the service lasted, but was not favoured with a sight
of the phenomenon, although others saw it cross the window
and return; and my friend, who knew it well, called my
attention to the fact for a moment, yet I could perceive

nothing.   I therefore left the place as unbelieving as ever, and supposed that I was either the victim of a hoax, or that it required a great stretch of imagination to fancy that a passing shadow was the required object.   However, not liking to discredit the statement of many friends, who were used to seeing it every Sunday, I consented on Easter Day to go to the same place and pew.   The seat I occupied was not an advantageous one, a large brass chandelier being between me and the lower panes of the window.   In the middle of the service, my eyes, which had hardly moved from the left or north side of the window, were attracted by a bright light formed like a female, robed and hooded, passing from north to south, with a rapid, gliding motion, outside the church, apparently at some distance.   The window is Gothic, and, I fancy, from 20 to 25 feet high, by 12 to 15 wide at the base.   The panes, through which the ghost shines, are about five feet high and about half-way between the top and bottom.   There are four divisions in the window, all of stained glass, of no particular pattern, the outer, on right and left, being of lighter colour than the two centre panes, and at the edge of each runs a rim of plain transparent glass about two inches wide, and adjoining the stone work. Through this rim especially could be seen what looked like a form transparent, but yet thick (if such a term can be used) with light.   It did not resemble linen for instance, but was far brighter, and would have been dazzling to a near observer. The robe was long and trailed.   The figure was, of course, not visible when it had crossed the window and passed behind the wall.   My friend whispered to me that it would return, must return, and at the end of five minutes or so the same figure glided back from right to left, having turned round while out of sight.   About half an hour later it again passed across from north to south, and having remained about ten seconds only, returned with what I believe to have been the figure of a young child, and stopped at the last pane but one, where both vanished. I did not see the child again, but a few seconds afterwards the woman re-appeared and completed the passage behind the last pane very rapidly. Nothing more was seen during the service, and no other opportunity presented itself to me for making observation. During each time the chandelier prevented me from obtaining a complete view, but there could be no doubt as to the shape, a certain amount of indistinctness however being caused by the stained glass. On the re-appearance for the last time I saw the head, which was, I believe, that of the child, move up and down distinctly, as if nodding. The figure shone with dazzling brightness, and appeared at a considerable distance, say thirty yards or so, though at the same time as distinct as possible, considering the obstruction of coloured glass. Each time, the level on which it glided was precisely the same, and afterwards, on carrying a straight line from the gallery in which I sat, through the part of the glass where the feet of the figure shone, and continuing that line (in my mind's eye, with all the objects before me except the ghost, whose position I had taken good notice of) I found that it would traverse a thick holly tree, eight or nine feet high, and would reach the ground itself in the middle of a gravel yard belonging to the back premises of the house, called the vicarage, at a distance of twelve or fifteen yards from the window. Any person walking between the window and the holly tree would hardly be seen at all, much less be seen in the place which the apparition occupies; and anyone on the further side of the tree, would be almost, if not quite invisible, on account of the holly and other bushes and the dead wall. Any one about there at all can easily be seen from the many houses on all sides. If it were a shadow thrown upon the glass of the window it would, of course, be seen by those in the gallery. It cannot be a reflection on the principle of Pepper's Ghost, which is produced by the figure actually being in a very strong light, and appearing reflected on glass

in a darkish spot. The lights both inside and outside of the
church at York, which might be thought to produce the
ghost, are precisely the reverse, and any figure required to be
reproduced by reflection on the east window would have to
be standing or walking in the centre of the aisle. For the
above facts I can vouch, and I have no reason to believe
that the following are either incorrect or exaggerated. It is
said to appear very frequently on Trinity Sunday, and to
bring two other figures on to the scene, another female,
called the nurse, and the child. It is often seen as distinctly
on a dark, rainy, or snowy day, as when the sun is shining.
When I saw it the sun was not bright. The motion is even,
not at all jerky. Sometimes it glides swiftly ; at other times
slowly. It cannot be a mere accidental reflection from a
door or window, for the figure faces different ways according
to the direction in which it is going ; and it is not always
alone, nor do the figures always act in concert. One of my
friends, with a companion, has watched outside on the wall
where he had a full view of the whole place around, during
morning service. The ghost has been seen from the inside,
while outside nothing was visible. It is said to have haunted
the church for 150, 200, and some authorities say 300 years,
and there are many pretty legends connected with it. One
of the many traditions says that 300 years ago, during
religious disturbances, a party of soldiers came to sack the
convent attached to this church, that the abbess, a woman
of great virtue and courage, stopped them as they were
entering, declaring that they should enter over her dead
body only, and that, should they succeed in their sacrilegious
purpose, as they afterwards did, her spirit would haunt the
place until the true church was re-established, and a convent
built on the same spot. Another story relates that during
the plague, some two hundred years ago, a nurse and child
died of the pestilence, and were necessarily buried outside the
city walls, while the unfortunate mother of the child, at her

death, was interred in Holy Trinity churchyard. Here the mother waits and receives the nurse and child, weeping and wringing her hands before parting with them. The same scene is often re-acted several times during the same day, and even during the same service. Whatever may have been the circumstances under which the ghost (if it is one, which is hard to believe in these matter-of-fact days) commenced its peculiar promenade, I would recommend those who have the chance to go to Holy Trinity Church, York, and see for themselves, though a sight of the apparition cannot always be assured. A ghost in broad daylight does no harm, frightens no one, and ought to interest everybody."

The following is an extract from the *Hull Advertiser* of 13th August, 1818, relative to an apparition seen in Skipsea Lane. A correspondent to that paper, on the date mentioned, says:—"About six months ago, a small party, including myself, having met at the house of a lady in Holderness, our conversation, in its range, happened to rest on the subject of supernatural appearances. The good lady of the house expressed her disbelief in the reality of such appearances, which led a gentleman of known veracity to relate what he himself had seen. About ten years ago, he said, as I was travelling on horseback, one afternoon in the month of March, on the road from Hornsea to Bridlington, just as I was ascending the brow of a hill on the south of Skipsea, I observed a woman, apparently young, dressed in white, walking a little before me, on my left hand, between the hedge and the road. Supposing that she had been visiting at a house on the top of the hill close by, I turned to see if there were any persons in attendance at the door, but it was shut, and none to be seen. My curiosity, being now greater than before, to know who this genteel person was, I followed her at the distance of twenty or thirty yards down the hill, one hundred or one hundred and fifty yards long, and expected when I got to the bottom, where there was a small brook, that I should meet her in attempting to gain the carriage bridge, forming the road ; but, to my great astonishment, when she approached the brook, instead of turning to the right to gain the bridge, she vanished from my sight at the very time my eyes were fixed upon her. As soon as I got home I related the strange affair to my family ; and as it was light, and I had not been previously thinking of apparitions, nor was I ever in the habit of speculating on such subjects, I am firmly persuaded that what I saw was one, although I never heard that there was anything ever seen there before or since. The lady of the house, who had listened with particular attention to this recital, said, at the conclusion of it, that what she had just heard had made a greater impression on her mind than anything she had ever heard before ; for, continued she, about five years ago I had a servant, who was a young man of good character, of a bold active disposition, and who professed a disbelief in any supernatural appearances. In the month of November, about Martinmas time, he requested leave to go to Bridlington, and also to be accommodated with a horse, which was granted him. Being desirous of making a long holiday of it, he rose early in the morning and set off two hours before daybreak ; but, to my great surprise, returned home early in the afternoon, before it was dark. On being questioned if anything was the matter with him, he replied that he had been so much alarmed that he was resolved never to travel in the dark if he could avoid it, ' For,' said he, ' as I was cantering along Skipsea Lane, in the morning, bending forwards with my face downwards, the horse suddenly bolted from the road to such a distance that I was very nearly dismounted. On recovering, and looking about to see what had affrighted the horse, I saw a fine lady, dressed in white, with something like a black veil on her face, standing close by. How I got to Skipsea I cannot tell, but I was so frightened that I durst go no further, but walked up and down the town until it was light, when I found some person going the same road, whom I accompanied to Bridlington.'"

This apparition is believed to be the ghost of the murdered wife of Drogo de Bevere, the first count of Holderness, whose castle was at Skipsea Brough, about half a mile away ; the keep of which stood on a large hill where may be seen one huge mass of cemented whinstones, all that is left of the actual building. The immense earthworks and wide moats still testify to the impregnable nature of this fortress.

No one has seen this ghost for years, but in the castle grounds there is a sort of pit, of which the boys of Skipsea say that if you walk round it seven times, Awd Molly (for that is her name) will come up dressed in white.

On the other side of Skipsea, at Skipsea Brough, along the Bail Welt, by the side of the enormous earthworks, the White Lady, headless, still takes her nightly walk, and breaks down all stiles and fences placed across her path. The last new stile was made remarkably firm and strong, and would test her powers of destruction to the utmost.

This neighbourhood is very ghostly. Between Atwick and Skipsea there races along occasionally the headless man, mounted on a swift horse; and between Atwick and Bewholme, at the foot of the hill on which Atwick church stands, there is a spring and pool of water, overhung by willows, haunted by the Halliwell Boggle.

A boggle is an imaginary hobgoblin, without any special form, causing fear or terror. The word is formed directly from the word "*bug*" a terror.

The bah-ghaist or bar-gest (*i.e.* bear ghost, bug bear) is a spectre which takes the form of a bear or black dog, with large flaming eyes as big as saucers, and whose appearance is a sign of death. Sometimes it howls at night round the house in which the fated person is.

A wimwam is an imaginary hobgoblin of minor order, and is applied to anything which causes fright.

Awd Goggie is a sprite which has charge of the orchards, and children are afraid to go there after dark, for fear Awd Goggie shall get them.

Between Frodingham and Foston a headless man haunts the road, but he has only been seen once, and that was by a man who had spent some hours at the public-house previous to leaving Foston. Behind him, on the same horse, this ghost rode, only leaving him when they reached Frodingham. There are people who say the man was drunk, but for all that they believe the road is haunted.

WHITE CROSS.

At White Cross, between Leven and Riston, a woman without a head used to be seen on the road and who leaped up behind horsemen and slapped their ears. The people were so terrified of going that way after dark, that they would sooner travel miles about than encounter her.

The boggle infesting Brigham Lane end, where four roads meet, is a white dog, known as Willie Sled's dog. Willie Sled used to attend to those who came to the Brigham sand-pit; and as nearly every pit in the Riding has its goblin, this one is named after him, who attended to the pit for so many years.

When bricklayers wish to give a reddish colour to the mortar, they use pounded bricks or tiles to mix with it. This powder is called simmon, and simmon pounding was formerly the hard labour punishment in Beverley Gaol, where there used to be a ghost having the name of Awd Simmon Beeather (Old Simmon Beater) and his appearance was dreaded by the criminals more than the confinement and punishment.

It was once the custom to bury suicides at cross roads, with a stake through their bodies, and such places are always accounted haunted. Horses especially are subject to the ghostly influence. A lady friend of mine, who at one time lived near such a place, declared that every horse which passed that way, either shied, stood stock still, bolted, trembled, or even wheeled round and refused to pass the place without being led.

The Hob Thrust, or Robin Round Cap, is a good natured fellow who assists servant maids by doing their work in the early morning. As he never wears clothes, it is told that one servant girl offered to make him a harden shirt (a shirt made of coarse, brown linen), but this gave him such offence that he instantly departed and never returned. Should he, however, have spite against any one, he annoys them terribly by breaking crockery, upsetting the milk, letting the beer run to waste, throwing down pans, rattling things together, and giving the place a reputation for being haunted. The Rev. W. H. Jones relates a story of a Holderness farmer who had his life made so miserable by one of these impish spirits that he determined to leave his farm. All was ready, and the carts, filled with furniture, moved away from the haunted house. As they went, a friend inquired " Is tha flitting " and before the farmer could reply, a voice came from the churn, " Ay, we're flitting !" and lo ! there sat Robin

Round Cap, who was also changing his residence. Seeing this, the farmer returned to his old home. By the aid of charms, Robin was enticed into a well, and there he is to this day, for the well is still called Robin Round Cap Well.

Near Flambrough is a circular hole, resembling a dry pond, in which a Flambro' girl committed suicide. It is believed that any one bold enough to run nine times round this place will see Jenny's spirit come out, dressed in white; but no one yet has been bold enough to venture more than eight times, for then Jenny's spirit called out—

> " Ah'll tee on me bonnet,
> An' put on me shoe,
> An' if thoo's nut off,
> Ah'll seean catch thoo!"

A farmer, some years ago, galloped round it on horseback, and Jenny did come out, to the great terror of the farmer, who put spurs to his horse and galloped off as fast as he could, the spirit after him. Just on entering the village, the spirit, for some reason unknown, declined to proceed farther, but bit a piece clean out of the horse's flank, and the old mare had a white patch there to her dying day.

What old hall and castle is there without its ghost or haunted chamber? In Watton Abbey a certain wainscotted room is said to be haunted, and the reason thereof is as follows. During the Civil Wars a lady and her infant secreted themselves in this room, to which access could be obtained by means of a narrow staircase, descending to the moat or stream which flows underneath the building. Her retreat was discovered by some ruffianly soldiers, who entered the room at dead of night by means of this secret entrance, and after murdering her and her infant, took possession of her jewels and valuables and then decamped.

This abbey is believed to have an underground passage to Beverley Minster, or as some say, to the "Lady Well" at

F

Kilnwick whose holy waters have been most powerful in working miraculous cures.

Mr. G—, a respectable Holderness farmer, resides in a mansion situated at a considerable distance from any other. He has been accustomed for several years, at intervals, to hear during the night the sounds of different instruments, which, together, produced a most delectable and harmonious concert. Two or three friends were taking their supper with him when a domestic came to inform them that the musicians were at work in the garden. The party immediately sallied out, and, although they could perceive nothing save trees loaded with snow, their ears were ravished with notes of music. The night was more than usually serene, the moon nearly full, and yet, notwithstanding a minute search, not the slightest vestige of a human being could be discovered. The music was all this time continued, and, as far as they could judge, within a few paces of the place they occupied. The farmer and his friends are convinced that they are indebted to "fairies" for the entertainment they received; and as that part of the country was formerly, according to oral tradition, the theatre often selected by Queen Mab and her tiny followers, to perform their mystic evolutions, and "Dance the Hay," they are induced to hope it is again fixed upon for the same purpose; and that times, like those in yore, are on the eve of returning. (The *Folk Lore Journal*, vol. v., p. 156).

About half way down the hill forming the eastern slope of Nafferton Slack, by the road-side, to prevent waggons leaving the roadway, stood a large stone, which was believed to have wonderful powers. At night, at certain seasons, it glowed like fire, sometimes it seemed but the portal of a well-lighted hall; and one old stone-breaker declared he had heard wonderful music issuing therefrom, the like of which he had never heard before; while on one occasion he had seen troops of gaily-dressed elfins repairing thither, some on foot and some in carriages, and they all went into this mysterious hall. The old man is dead, the stone is gone, and the fairies have departed.

An old lady, with whom I formerly lodged, when returning home, and while in the country, one moonlight night, saw a company of fairies dancing round the trunk of an oak tree. She was looked upon as a friend, (for did she not possess superhuman power?) but the little folk suddenly disappeared, on the approach of some one on horseback.

In a field on the road side, just before reaching Wold Newton from Bridlington, is a large mound, about 300 feet in circumference and 60 feet in height. It is called "Willey How," and has been supposed to be inhabited by fairies. A singularly odd legend is told in connection with this relic of bygone days. One day a rustic of Wold Newton went on a visit to the neighbouring village of North Burton. The love of beer kept him till late at night. On his return, the night being dark, as he neared the "Willey How," great was his astonishment to hear merry sounds proceed from it— sounds of feasting and singing. Wondering who could have come to that lonely spot to enjoy themselves at such an hour, he approached the mound, and for the first time he beheld a door in its side. Being well mounted, he rode close to it, looked through, and beheld a spacious apartment, filled with a magnificent company of both sexes, at a sumptuous feast. One of the cupbearers approached, and offered him the cup to drink from, according to the etiquette of fairy life, which if he drank of, he would immediately lose all consciousness and be carried into fairy land. Our rustic, however, was too much for the fairies. He poured out every drop of the contents, and galloped off with the cup. The fairy banqueters rushed from their feast and gave chase. But his horse was swift of foot, and by a miracle he reached his home in safety and secured the valuable prize. This event having reached the ears of the king, the cup, which was of unknown material, and equally strange in form and colour, was presented to him.

CHAPTER VII.

Charms, Spells, and Divination.

FROM all ages, man has striven to peep into futurity, and endeavoured to read that which is wisely hidden from him. What this life shall be, and when it shall end, have ever been disquieting factors in human life, and strange methods have been adopted to discover one or both.

Watching in the church porch on St. Mark's Eve, to see, entering the church, the forms of all those who were to die during the ensuing year, used to be a common practice. When, as at Leven and North Frodingham, the church was about a mile from the village, it was only a person of the strongest nerves who could travel that lonely road at midnight.

Fortune-tellers went, or acquired the reputation of going, thus to watch, so that their patrons might be informed if they were to die soon. Doubtless, a liberal fee procured the desired information.

Old Peg Doo (Margaret Dove), many years ago, used to watch on St. Mark's eve, in the north porch of the Priory Church, Bridlington, and there saw all the forms of those who were to die during the year. The divulging of the information thus obtained formed a considerable income, for the fearful ones were glad to pay for the pleasure of knowing they had to live another year, and the fated ones had time to set their affairs in order.

Another method of peeping into futurity was termed "caff-riddling," and was thus practised on St. Mark's Eve. The barn doors were set wide open, and at midnight the prying ones were to commence riddling the chaff. Should the riddler be doomed to die within the year, two persons would pass by the open door, carrying a coffin.

Near Malton, some years ago, two men and a woman went to riddle caff on St. Mark's Eve. The two men riddled, but nothing was seen. Then the woman began to riddle, and scarcely had the chaff begun to fall on the floor, when they all saw the ominous pair of coffin-bearers pass by. The men rushed out to look, but all had disappeared, there was nothing in sight. History does not record the sequel, but, of course, the woman died.

The Holy Bible is frequently used as a charm, and, in moments of doubt or perplexity, its sacred pages are opened at random, while the perplexed one, with eyes averted or closed, places his finger on the open page. The verse or passage thus chosen is taken as an indication of the course of action which is to be pursued.

Such is the power of the Lord's Prayer that to repeat it backwards will bring into sight his Satanic majesty himself.

The superstitious among men, in order to see their future love, would hie them to the fairy stones, * at Burdale, and there, with the full moon brightly shining, at midnight, would see the one who should be all the world to them.

---

* These stones are perfectly natural—a breccia formed of flint and chalk fragments, collected in a rift in the chalk rock—cemented together by its own siliceous cement, and so hard as to resist ordinary denudation, while its original chalk surrounding has been dissolved. —*Rev. E. M. Cole, M.A.*

To divine the pride of any one, take a hair belonging to that person, and pull it smartly between the nails of thumb and finger, and the pride is in accordance with the curled appearance of the hair after the operation.

The first new moon in the New Year must be viewed by a young woman, through a silk handkerchief, and the number of moons shewing through it represents the number of moons (months) she will remain un-married. During this operation, the following rhyme is recited :—

> " New moon, new moon, I hail thee,
> This night my true-love for to see !
> Not in grand or rich array,
> But in the dress he wore this day."

in the belief that the said true-love will appear that night in a dream. If this charm fail, another can be tried, viz :—Walk backwards upstairs to bed, undress with the back to the bed, get into bed backwards, lie on your back, and then—to sleep and dream.

If the fire burn badly and draw ill there must be evil influence at work, which must be counteracted by placing the poker upright against the bars thus making a cross, and lo ! the fire recovers its required brightness, to enable three or four girls to place nuts on the top bar, which nuts represent themselves and their sweethearts. If the nuts remain together, and are consumed, all is well ; but if they fly apart, alack-a-day !

During the heating of the nuts a flake of soot has formed on the top bar. Its presence there indicates the coming of a stranger, and a man too. If it had been on the second bar, it would have indicated a strange woman. As it sways to and fro in the draught they watch it intently. Where will it fall ? If it fall on the hearth, woe ! for—

> " A stranger on the floor,
> Is a beggar at your door."

but should it fall into the fire, then, well! for—

> " A stranger in the fire,
>   Is one that you desire."

Some read the omen differently; if the "stranger" fall on the hearth, the visitor will call the same day; but if it go into the fire, the strange caller will not come that day.

Horse shoes are still frequently nailed to stable doors to keep witches out, and ward off their influence. Though much of the belief is dead, yet we find the idea preserved in Christmas and New Year cards, in brooches, scarf pins, studs, and solitaires; and such articles are chosen as being " lucky."

Thin flat oolite stones, having a natural perforation, are found in abundance on the Yorkshire coast. They are termed " witch steeans" (stones), and are tied to door-keys, or suspended by a string behind the cottage door, "to keep witches out." Mr. Thos. Holderness, Driffield, says :—" I remember Jinny Jewison, an old woman who kept a mangle, and sold butter-scotch, in Kirkgate, Bridlington, having one of these stones hung behind her cottage door, with which she would not have parted on any account." As a relic of this custom, a reel, from which the cotton has been used, is often tied on bunches of keys.

When anyone sneezes it is customary to say " Bless us!" or " Bless the bairn!" in order to charm away the ill-luck which would ensue.

When a child's tooth comes out, it ought not to be thrown away, or the child would have to seek the lost tooth after death. The tooth should be dropped into the fire, and the following incantation recited :—

> " Fire, fire, tak a beean (bone),
>   An' send oor——* a good teeath ageean." (tooth again).

At Christmas time, when stirring the plum pudding, you

* Insert child's name.

must wish your dearest wish, but not express it, or the wish will not come true.

Warts can either be cured or charmed away. The writer once had a row of warts, thirteen in number. He was told by an aged dame, as she sat crouching on a three-legged stool, smoking a short black pipe, before her cottage door, to take thirteen bad peas and throw them over his left shoulder, never heeding where they went, all the while repeating some incantation, which has been forgotten.

Some wart-charmers, however, professed to have direct influence over these excrescences. A young man, whose hands were nearly covered with warts, was told by one of these men that he was very foolish to be so disfigured, when it was such an easy matter to get rid of the warts. "How?" asked he. "Oh! I can charm them away." The young fellow was sceptical, and scouted the idea. "Then," said the charmer, to shew his power, "choose one that you will not have removed, and I will take away all the rest." One was chosen in the middle of the back of the left hand, and, in the course of a few days, every one had disappeared, save the wart chosen to be the positive evidence of the charmer's power— a power which he divulged to no one.

A sty on the eye can be charmed away by rubbing it gently with the finger ring of a young unmarried lady.

When any fruit, such as plums, &c., containing stones, is eaten at table, the stones are used afterwards to tell fortunes with. Placing them all together, the owner, on whose plate they are, moves them away one by one, saying :—

> "This year, next year,
> Sometime, never,"

thus moving four stones, during the repetition of the doggerel verse. The word or phrase used with the removal of the last stone indicates the time when the young woman will be married, or the young man become rich.

If when shelling peas you find a pod containing nine peas, you must throw it over your shoulder, and wish, and your wish will come true. Divination by peascod is alluded to by Gay,—

> " As peascod once I plucked, I chanced to see
> One that was closely filled with three times three ;
> Which, when I cropp'd, I safely home conveyed,
> And o'er the door, the spell in secret laid.
> The latch moved up, when who should first come in,
> But in his proper person—Lubberkin!"

CHAPTER VIII.

Witches and Witchcraft.

"Double, double, toil and trouble."
Macbeth, iv. 1

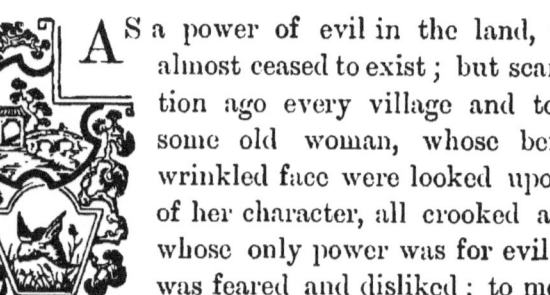AS a power of evil in the land, the witch has almost ceased to exist; but scarcely a generation ago every village and town contained some old woman, whose bent form and wrinkled face were looked upon as an index of her character, all crooked and awry; and whose only power was for evil; a being who was feared and disliked; to meet whom was fraught with danger, necessitating the crossing of the road, or turning down another lane or street.

Woman fares badly in folk-lore. Her presence often foretold ill-luck, and old age brought only fear and torment, which were only partly compensated by her "evil eye." Any sudden, unaccountable sickness, either in man or beast, was surely laid to the charge of a witch, to discover whom the aid of the wise man was invoked, but not always with success. A story is related of some one going to consult the wise man with regard to a sudden illness, and, in order to discover who had cast the evil eye, he told them, among other things to make a large fire in every room in the house, and roast a sheep's heart before the fire in the bedroom of the sick man. In that room they were to remain until the witch came to the house, willy-nilly. While there congregated, some of the fire in a lower room fell out of the firegrate, set fire to the house, and the patient barely escaped with life.

The power of the wise man or woman was called into requisition as a detective is cases of theft; and as a terrible something with which to frighten children into speaking the truth. If a boy was suspected of stealing, and he denied the impeachment, he was told they would "fetch wise man tiv him, an *he knew*," which threat was sufficient, if the boy were guilty.

Forty or fifty years ago, J. S., of Haisthorpe, was credited with wonderful wisdom and skill, and exercised magical powers in the northern part of East Yorkshire. By his magic he healed a woman at Specton, who had been bed-ridden for years. Such was the effect of this faith-healing, as he called it, that it aroused an almost religious frenzy, and the healed woman and her friends, for three successive Sundays, formed a procession through the streets of Bridlington, singing all the while, to give thanks for the wonderful cure.

A lady, who lived in Holderness, being suddenly seized with illness, whereby she lost the use of her legs, was declared by him to be bewitched, and he having, by his power, discovered the witch, foretold that when the witch died the lady would recover. The witch soon died, and, of course, the prophecy came true.

Dr. R. Wood, Driffield, thus writes:—"A few years ago one of the residents in the village of Kirkburn had long been ailing, and other calamities befell him—such as the sudden death of his old mare, &c.—and, one Saturday night, whilst he and his wife were sitting by the fireside, the kitchen clock was distinctly heard to send forth a moaning sound. His suspicions were at once awakened as to the true cause of these various afflictions; and fixed themselves upon a certain

person (of course, a woman), whom he regarded as the
guilty individual. A wise man (the J.S. mentioned above)
was fortunately at hand, for he lived only a few miles away,
and was brought to the place of destination in a carrier's cart.
Towards midnight the ceremonies began. First, some
chapters were read out of the Bible; the Lord's Prayer was
read backwards, together with a series of other similar
solemnities. A black hen was then brought upon the scene,
and the heart taken out, whilst the poor bird was partly
alive. This was stuck full of pins. The whole party then
went into the garden, where a hole was dug in the ground,
and the fowl put in.

"The master of the ceremonies had sagaciously provided
himself with some 'fizzing stuff,' which, when water was
poured on it, and sundry adjurations had been addressed to
the evil one, began to boil up with such fury as to drive the
poor man and his wife back into the house in a state of great
trepidation and alarm.

"The carrier himself, who had probably charged himself
with some Dutch courage before starting, was disposed at
first to question the power and skill of his travelling companion, but was somewhat awe-stricken, when, upon arrival
at a lonely spot, the magician offered to bring forth the
prince of darkness himself, if any desire to see him was felt.
'Nay!' the man replied, 'I have tried to keep him off me
all my life, and I do not want to see him now.'" Dr. Wood
adds:—"This statement was made to me by the carrier
himself."

S. G., of Driffield, was famous all over the country side as
a wise woman and fortune-teller. Very, very numerous are
the people who have gone to her to have their fortunes told,
to have the result of their enterprise foretold, or to consult
her as to the wisdom of certain intended speculations.
Maidens went to know if their love-affairs would prosper;
anxious ones went to enquire if their forms had entered the

church porch, which was only a short distance in front of the
wise woman's house, and there she watched on St. Mark's
Eve ; tradesmen might be seen there after dark, to know if
their business would improve under certain alterations ; and
fearful mothers enquired if their absent children were well
and prosperous, for there was no penny post then, and few
could write, even if there had been cheap postage, and if the
fates were propitious they might have some vision of the
absent one, which sent them away rejoicing.

Had we been there some seventy-five years ago, we might
have seen a well-to-do farmer come ambling on his grey mare
up to the door of the cottage. His face wore an anxious look,
for he had had stolen from him a bag containing a hundred
guineas. All efforts to discover the thief had been unsuccessful, so he had ridden from Skipsea to consult the famous
woman.   He enters, and shortly re-appears looking greatly
relieved, as she has told him not to trouble about his loss, for
the money would shortly be returned to him, but if not
before next week, he must visit her again.

Before the man reached Driffield all Skipsea knew his
errand, and the self-convicted thief felt that discovery was
certain ; so, when the farmer arose next morning, he found
the bag, with the hundred guineas in it, hanging on the
door sneck, where it had been placed by the thief during
the night.

This wise woman afterwards lived in Eastgate, Driffield,
and children were afraid to go along the narrow lane for fear
of meeting her.   When she died "she flew ower Driffield
chotch (church) on a blazin' besom." Whither away, gossips
do not say.

About twenty years ago, there dwelt in Little Queen
Street, Hull, a little man, deaf and dumb, who was known
as a " planet ruler," to whom business men resorted frequently
for advice. A lady thus describes a visit made by her and
a lady friend, and, for the information given thereat, half-a-

crown was paid :—"We soon found the little house, and a waiting woman ushered us into a small room, where the "planet ruler" sat at a table covered with large folio volumes, and having in front of him a slate and pencil, and a card on which the alphabet was printed in capital letters. Beckoning us to him, he pointed quickly to certain letters which spelt DATE OF BIRTH; and we wrote down the required date on the slate. He then opened one of his huge volumes, which we saw were in black letter, searched for something therein, closed the book, and taking the slate and pencil in his hand, pointed rapidly to the letters on the card; and these letters, put into words, told me that my mother was dead, and my father was married again to a lady with fair hair; that I had two brothers, one older and one younger than myself, and that the older one was married; that I had two sisters, both older than myself, and one of them was married; that I had two lovers, both named G (for George) but that I should marry neither of them. He then looked me closely in the face, and told me that if I did not take care I should have a serious illness. Everything he told me was correct, and his prophecies came true. After each item he looked up enquiringly, and I signified by a nod of the head that it was correct. No word was spoken on *either* side, and the only question he asked was the date of my birth; but if I failed to understand his pointing, so that it had to be repeated, he shewed great irritation. The whole affair was so uncanny that what we had undertaken as a girlish freak became a very serious thing, and made a lasting impression on us both."

Old Nanny Rowley, Weaverthorpe, was greatly feared as a witch. A man, against whom she had a spite, was passing her house, driving a horse with a heavy load, but, when opposite her door, there it stood stationary, in spite of all the efforts of the horse. He was sure she had bewitched it, and, thinking that affairs had now reached a crisis, he rushed into the house and struck her on the cheek, causing the blood to flow. This put an end to her power, and the horse was able to proceed with the load.

At Bridlington, Rebecca Hird used to tell fortunes, chiefly to women who were anxious not to die old maids ; but women of most respectable position used to consult her.

Poor old Nanny Thrusk, whose little thatched cottage was the last of the departed village of Bonwick, had the reputation of possessing an evil eye. She had done penance in Skipsea Church more than once, arrayed in a white sheet and holding a candle in her hand. On one occasion some mischievous lads were driving away her donkey, secretly and in fear, but Nanny came out, saw them, and transfixed them with the power of her eye, and there they stood, helpless and immoveable, until she released them.

From the *Depositions from York Castle*,* under the date October 14th, 1654, it is said :—"Elizabeth Roberts, wife of a joiner at Beverley, was charged with witchcraft. John Greencliffe said that on Saturday last, about seven in the evening, Elizabeth Roberts did appeare to him in her usuall wearing clothes, with a ruff about her neck, and presently vanishing, turned herself into the similitude of a catt, which fixed close about his leg, and after much struggling, vanished, whereupon he was much pained at his heart. Upon Wednesday there seized a catt upon his body, which did strike him on the head, upon which he fell into a swound or trance. After he received the blow he saw the said Elizabeth escape upon a wall, in her usuall wearing apparell. Upon Thursday she appeared unto him in the likness of a bee, which did very much afflict him, to wit in throwing of his body from place to place, notwithstanding there were five or six persons to hold him down."

A curious anecdote is related of Lord Chief Justice Holt. When a young man, he, with companions who were law

* Surtees Society. Vol. 40, p. 67.

students like himself, ran up a score at an inn, which they were not able to pay. Mr. Holt observed that the landlord's daughter looked very ill, and, posing as a medical student, asked what ailed her, when he was informed she suffered from ague. Mr. Holt, continuing to play the doctor, gathered sundry herbs, mixed them with great ceremony, rolled them up in parchment, scrawled some characters on the same, and, to the great amusement of his companions, tied it round the neck of the young woman, who, straightway, was cured of her ague. After the cure, the pretending doctor offered to pay the bill, but the grateful landlord would not consent, and allowed the party to leave the house with hearts as light as their pockets.

Many years after, when on the Bench, a woman was brought before him accused of witchcraft. She denied the charge, but said she had a wonderful ball which never failed to cure the ague. The charm was handed to the judge, who recognized it as the very ball he had made for the young woman at the inn, to relieve him and his companions out of a difficult position. *

* Records of York Castle, p. 230.

CHAPTER IX.

Place Nicknames, Rhymes and Sayings.

THOUGH we cannot raise a cry of 'Town' or 'Gown,' yet the town dwellers have nicknames for the country dwellers, and the latter return the compliments with interest. Of this class are—bahn deear savidge (barn door savage); cunthry hawbuck; fahmer joskin; clod kicker; boily (from boiled milk being used for breakfast); off-cunthry-chaps (men from a distance); coonther loupers (counter jumpers); etc. As will be seen, Place Bye-names are given either from the produce of the place, from some notorious deed, or from some notorious person connected therewith. Some are harmless, some humourous, and others only perpetuate that which never merited remembrance.

Of sayings applicable to the county, the Yorkshireman's Arms are said to be a flea, a fly, a magpie, and a flitch of bacon; because a flea will bite anyone; a fly will drink with anyone; a magpie will talk with anyone; and a flitch of bacon is no good till it is hung, all of which are supposed to be applicable to a Yorkshireman.

Horses and Yorkshiremen are inseparable, for is it not

G

said that if you shake a bridle over his grave, he will rise and
steal a horse to put in it; while if you give him a horse, he
will soon find a halter.

Though 'Tyke' (a dog) is a common epithet for the people
of Yorkshire, the following assigns the dog to Berkshire :—

" Hampshire hog,
Berkshire dog,
Yorkshire bite,
London white (wight)."

When George IV. said to Jemmy Hirst, " So you are a
Yorkshire bite?" Jemmy replied " Yes, but not for thee ! "
and though the term signifies keenness in the way of over-
reaching, it probably had its origin in the proverbial Yorkshire hospitality, which decreed " You mun hev a bite o'
summat afooar y'u gan," and that meant the best the house
could provide.

Sancton was a place famous for cock-fighting, the sport
being under the special patronage of the clergyman, of whom
it is related that, reversing the usual order of things, he fell
asleep during the singing of a long psalm, and, on being
awakened by the clerk, cried out " All right, a guinea on
black cock! Black cock a guinea." Hence the Sancton
people, especially the worse lot, are known as Sancton Cockins.

The last man executed on Hornsea Gibbet bore the name
of Pennell; so that name is given to the poaching, loafing
set of vagabonds about the place, who are called Hornsea
Pennells.

Similarly, owing to an extensive robbery of bacon by a
Cranswick man, Cranswick Bacon became the bye-name for
the people of this village; but so angrily is this resented,
that I have seen railway carriage windows broken by the
natives, because some traveller uttered the offensive word.
Of this place it is said, there was only one honest man in
Cranswick, and he stole a saddle.

PATRINGTON CHURCH.

(THE QUEEN OF HOLDERNESS).

Patrington Church is the Queen of Holderness, and right worthily it merits the name; but, owing to so many of its vicars dying shortly after their appointment, it has acquired a bad name, "Patrington kill priest." The present popular vicar (Rev. H. E. Maddock, M.A.) told me that, shortly after his arrival, he enquired of his parishoners if they knew of such a saying, and they replied that it was well known, but they had not told him for fear of disheartening him. The clock on this church came from Louth (Lincs), where its incorrect time-keeping gave rise to a proverb, "As false as Louth clock;" and even now, one of its two faces always shews the time one hour and five minutes before the other. A native of this place, having no exalted opinion of his fellow townsmen, is reported to have said "For feeals (fools) an' thick heeads cum ti Pathrinton."

The splendid pile of St. Augustine's, Hedon, grand in its altered fortunes, is the King of Holderness.*

A riddle, common to the district of the villages therein mentioned, runs as follows :—

> "Buckton, Bempton,
> Reighton, Speeton,
> All begin(s) with A."

The people of Speeton are known as 'Speeton Rangers,' and they of Buckton and Bempton as 'Buckton Hawny'ns,' and 'Bempton Hawny'ns.'

Great Kelk is built on one side of the road, so of it, it is said :—

> "Great Kelk, where God never dwelt,
> And honest man never rode through it."

another saying is :—"The devil cannot ride through Great Kelk." He can only ride past it.

Howsham is built similarly, so it has given rise to the

* See frontispiece.

proverb :—" All of a side like Hoosam." Another place
proverb is :—" All of a muck-heeap, like Howden Fair ;" or
" All of an uproar, like Howden Fair."   A comparison used
locally, is to say that one thing is better than another, as, York
is better than Full Sutton ; while Nafferton is the place
where it is said " They shoe pigs."

At Cottingham are some intermittent springs, in Keldgate,
and these are said to be dependent on the river Derwent, 20
miles away ; so

> " When Derwent flows,
>   Then Kel'gate goes."

As Cottingham largely produces vegetables to supply Hull
Market, the people are styled " Cottingham Tonnups."

Paull church stands about a quarter of a mile from the
village, hence :—

> " High Paull and Low, Paull and Paull Holme,
>   There never was a fair maid married at Paull town."

Burlington, otherwise Bridlington, is situated at the head
of a beautiful bay, bearing the same name, to the south
of Flambrough Head.   The name is vulgarly pronounced
Bolliton.

Many years ago, a number of workmen were busily
engaged in repairing the roof of the grand old Priory
Church, one of the oldest parish churches in the East Riding.
For this purpose, a long beam of timber was required, which
had to be taken into the church, in order to be hoisted up
to the roof.   It was hauled to the richly-ornamented
western entrance, when its length was found to be much
greater than the width of the doorway.· Here things were
brought to a standstill, and the perplexing question arose,
" How are we to get the beam into the church ?" They set
their wits to work, and one suggested that they should saw

the beam in two; another suggested that they should cut a few feet off from each end; and a third proposed that they should knock a few stones out of each side of the doorway to make an opening sufficiently wide to admit it.

At the time of the dissolution of the monastic portion of this grand old Priory, in 1539, the two western towers, and probably the whole of the western façade of the church were being rebuilt, the workmen being busily engaged in the work when the commissioners arrived and commenced the demolition of the monastic portion of the edifice, consisting of the choir, the two transepts, the central tower, &c. This put an end to the erection of the west-end of the church, which had just reached the level of the roof, and the two western towers were not erected until. the complete restoration of the entire fabric, a few years ago, the north-west angle of the church remaining from 1539 till that time, as much a ruin as the old Abbeys and Monasteries so plentifully scattered over the country. In the interior of the church the arches of this tower were walled up, with the *debris* of the monastic buildings, cutting it completely off from the rest of the edifice. In this north-western angle, popularly known as "The Awd Steeple," the lapse of nearly three-and-a-half centuries, with the total absence of much-needed reparation, had made gaps and crevices, which were the resorts of owls, jackdaws, starlings, and other birds that made their nests and reared their young there.

While the workmen were busily suggesting their various schemes for getting the beam into the church, one of them looked up to this "Awd Steeple," and observed a jackdaw, which was building its nest there, fly into one of the crevices, with the end of a long straw in its mouth, which it dragged in. Observing this, he suddenly exclaimed, "Did ya see that, lads! That jackdaw tewk that sthraw in endways on. Let's see if this beeam 'll gan in seeam way." His mates were struck with the inspiration. They turned the beam end-wise, and got it into the church without further difficulty. From that time to the present, all natives of Bridlington have been facetiously called " Bolliton Jackdaws."

The three letters, B. B. B., forming the Bridlington coat of arms, are read as forming the initials of the phrase, Bad, Beggarly Bolliton ; though the former adjective is applied to the Quay, in a school-boy rhyme, which says of Bridlington, " Bolliton bonny lass." Akin to the " Scarborough Warning," is to threaten to give anyone " Bolliton."

Beverley Buffs is the name given to the soldiers at Beverley, because the facings of the Beverley Volunteer regimentals were buff. Their original colours now hang in the Percy Chapel, Beverley Minster.

When any one has his hair cropped very short, it is said " He's got a Beverley crop," because of the close cut the prisoners receive in Beverley Gaol, the prison for the Riding.

Hull people are known as Hull bulldogs, but this name is prevalent throughout the Riding. The beggar's Litany kept Hull in remembrance,

> " From Hull, Hell, and Halifax
> Good Lord, deliver us."

Elland is a few miles from Halifax, and it, with Hull and Halifax, possessed a gibbet, and all had stringent laws against pilfering, &c. Another rhyme refers to Hull,

> " When Dighton is pulled down,
> Hull shall become a great town."

Deighton is a small village about 5 miles S.E. of York, but some think Dighton is a mistake for Myton, which is now incorporated as a ward in the borough of Kingston-upon-Hull.

Taylor, the Water Poet, who visited Hull in 1622, says :—

> " There at mine Inne, each Night I tooke mine ease ;
> And there I gat a Cantle of Hull Cheese."

He adds, in a footnote :—"Hull cheese is much like a loafe
out of a Brewer's Basket. It is composed of two simples,
Mault and Water, in one compound, and is Cousin Germane
to the mightiest ale in England."

A local rhyme runs thus :—

> " Hornsea steeple, when I built thee,
>   Thou was' 10 miles off Burlington,
>   10 miles off Beverley, and 10 miles off sea."

The last clause is probably 01 mile off sea. There is now
no steeple to Hornsea Church. It was blown down in 1732,
and has never been rebuilt.

Instead of saying "You go to Jericho," the local equiva-
lent is "Thoo gan ti Hummer" (thou go to Humber).

Otherin' is a well-known dialect word, meaning slow-
witted; and the village of Ottringham (pronounced Otther-
ingham) is often said by sarcastic neighbours to have got its
name from its *otherin* inhabitants.

The local pronunciation of Ridgmont is Rijiment; while
Thorngumbald becomes twisted into Gum-bu-thorn.

The following are from Hazlitt's *English Proverbs.*

> " Oxford for learning,
>   London for wit,
>   Hull for women,
>   York for a tit." (p. 326).

> " Lincoln was, and London is,
>   And York shall be
>   The fairest city of the three." (p. 275).

> " If you go to Nunkilling,
>   You shall find your belly filling
>   Of whig or of whey ;
>   Go to Swine,
>   And come betime,
>   Or else you go empty away ;
>   But the Abbot of Meaux,
>   Doth keep a good hoose
>   By night and by day." (p. 234).

CHAPTER X.

Hero Tales.

" A Yorkshire bite ? "
" Aye ! but not for thee ! "

IT has been truly said, that, in Yorkshire, every other man you meet is a character; and this force of character, which often shews itself by its eccentricity, has produced many men of sterling worth, whose worthiness is known and acknowledged far beyond the confines of their own county.

SIR TATTON SYKES.

No account of the worthies of East Yorkshire would be complete, that did not, among many others, include the late Sir Tatton Sykes, of Sledmere. This broad-acred shire has produced many good men and true, but none whose name will linger with more enduring fame than that of the grand old master of Sledmere, who died on the 21st of March, 1863, in his 92nd year.

For more than half a century there was no face or figure more familiar to those who frequented the great northern race meetings, than that of Sir Tatton Sykes, who was regarded by 'Tykes' of high and low degree with feelings

MONUMENT TO THE LATE SIR TATTON SYKES.

(FROM A PHOTOGRAPH BY M. BOAK, DRIFFIELD).

of respect and veneration as deep as those which a tribe of Arabs entertains for its patriarchal Sheikh.

To the end of his days Sir Tatton was a man of great hardihood, of the most frugal tastes, and the most simple habits. It was his custom all his life to be up with the lark in the summer, and long before the sun in winter. His favourite breakfast was an apple tart and a hearty draught of new milk, and after he had partaken of that humble meal, he has often been known to relieve a stone breaker at his work by the roadside, and keep himself warm by breaking stones, until the man who has been sent to the Manor-house to be served with a pint of home-brewed, and a crust of bread, returned. No one, not even the poorest beggar, was ever known to leave that hospitable roof without at least a substantial 'crust' and a pint of the generous malt.

In physique, Sir Tatton was a splendid specimen of a stalwart Yorkshireman. He stood just six feet in his stockings, and though he, in his prime, never exceeded eleven stones, was remarkably muscular, and, as a boxer, was renowned for his terrifically hard hitting. In proof of this assertion we may adduce the following anecdote. Once when Sir Tatton was out on one of his sheep-buying expeditions, (sheep breeding was one of his hobbies), he ordered a 'pitcher of ale' at the bar of an inn. There was a couple of big bullying drovers lounging in the tap room, and one of these ruffians coolly took up the ale and drank it. Sir Tatton said not a word, but in his mild, quiet voice, ordered another draught, whereupon the second drover, with a brutal laugh, laid hands on it and tossed it off; a third supply was handed to the baronet, and when he had quaffed it, he quietly buttoned up his coat, told ruffian No. 1 to stand up, thrashed him to his heart's content, and then turning round to No. 2, who was somewhat amazed, and enraged at the discomfiture of his comrade, served him in precisely the same manner; after which, bruised and bleeding, the hulking bullies slunk away like whipped curs.

Sir Tatton's face was singularly pleasing, frank, open, honest, handsome. As a jockey he had few equals. In 1817, he rode to Aberdeen from Sledmere, with his racing jacket under his waistcoat, a clean shirt and a razor in his pocket, and after winning the Welter Stakes there, reached Doncaster in time to see the St. Leger run. The 720 miles were done in six days, on a little blood mare, that, with the exception of a little stiffness, seemed none the worse for the feat, done in so quiet and unostentatious a manner.

He will always be remembered as a pioneer of agriculture on the Wolds. Noticing on spots near his kennels, where bones had been scattered, that the grass grew more luxuriantly than elsewhere, he experimented with bones as a manure, visited Sheffield, and bought the waste dust from the knife-handle grinders; and, though laughed at, he lived long enough to see bone-dust extensively used as manure.

As a master of fox-hounds, Sir Tatton must hold a first rank. Not until he was 70, having been M.F. for forty years, did he resign the mastership.

The reverence of all classes for him amounted almost to idolatry. "How's Sir Tatton looking?" was the common question on the race days at York, Malton, Beverley, and Doncaster; and when he died, the mourning was deep and sincere. A Yorkshireman was once asked what were the three things best worth seeing in the county, and replied "York Minster, Fountains Abbey, and Sir Tatton;" but thinking there was too much of the church in his answer, amended it by saying "On second thoughts, I'll take out Abbey and put in Voltigeur."

Until death, he adhered to one style of dress—a long frock-coat, drab breeches, top boots, and frilled shirt—and when on one occasion a political chameleon was making fun of the antique style of the aged baronet's dress, Sir Tatton replied, "Yes, my lord, I wear the coat of my early days, but you change yours so frequently that I scarcely know you."

On Garton Hill top stands a beautiful monument, erected to his memory, by friends, tenants and admirers; and this monument forms a prominent feature in the landscape for miles around.

DICK NAP.

What stirring times were the Parliamentary elections at Beverley before the disfranchisement, and what election was complete without Dick Nap, who was a staunch supporter of John Wharton, of Skelton Castle, the representative of the borough for 36 years.

Dick Nap (Richard Sissons) gained his livelihood by collecting 'hoss muck' in the street, and, at election times, had his barrow painted orange (Wharton's colour); while ever and anon he raised his voice and shouted "Wharton for ivver!" Though so very, very poor, he was impervious to bribes; and only those who knew the Beverley of that day can form an idea of what that means. It is said that some of Wharton's supporters went to Dick's poor dwelling in order to test his loyalty. "Now, Mr. Nap, we want you to vote for the Conservative candidate!" "No! Wharton for ivver!" "But, Mr. Nap, you are a poor man, what say you to five sovereigns!" (laying the shining coins on the table). "No! Wharton for ivver!" "But, see what a lot you could buy with this money! Come now, will ten do?" (and the glittering row was doubled in length). His wife was overcome by the sight, and nudging him, said "Tak it, thoo feeal!" Dick turned to her, and sweeping his arm round, said, "Get thee behind me, Satan!" Then, turning to his tempters, he once more said "No! Wharton for ivver!" The bribe was doubled again, and twenty bright golden sovereigns lay on the plain wooden table, in that squalid room ; lay there for the poverty-stricken man's acceptance, but they were not taken, his refusal finding expression in his old cry " No ! Wharton for ivver !" He was faithful to the last, and was buried, wrapped in an orange coloured flag.

WILLIAM BRADLEY.

East Yorkshire has produced its giant as well as its dwarf —contrasts in more ways than one. William Bradley, the giant, measuring seven feet nine inches in height, and Edwin Calvert, the dwarf, only thirty six inches. The former a total abstainer, while the latter killed himself by excessive drinking, when only seventeen years of age.

William Bradley, a native of Market Weighton, weighed twenty seven stones when nineteen. His shoe was fifteen inches long and five and a half inches broad ; his stockings three feet nine inches from top to toe ; his walking stick five feet ten inches in length ; and his coffin nine feet long and three feet in breadth.

If children at play lost their ball in a spout, or on a house top, and they were unable to get it down, they would shout with glee on the appearance of Bradley, " Oh ! here's Bill Bradley coming, he'll get it down for us."

Such a prodigy must needs travel and exhibit himself. He had the honour of presentation to George IV., from whom he received a massive gold chain, which he valued highly and wore until his dying day.

On exhibiting himself at Hull Fair, in 1815, he issued a small hand-bill, of which the following is a copy :—" To be seen during the fair, at the house, No. 10, Queen Street, Mr. Bradley, the most wonderful and surprising Yorkshire Giant, 7 feet 9 inches high, weighs 27 stones ; who has had the honour of being introduced to their Majesties and Royal Family at Windsor, where he was most graciously received. A more surprising instance of gigantic stature has never been beheld, or exhibited in any other kingdom ; being proportionate in all respects, the sight of him never fails to give universal gratification, and will fill the beholder's eyes with wonder and astonishment. He is allowed by the greatest judges to surpass all men ever yet seen. Admittance One Shilling !"

Having retired, with a competency, he had a special house, with rooms sufficiently lofty and a tall entrance, built for him in Northgate, Market Weighton, where he resided till his death in 1820.

The house is still standing, but has since been converted into shops. One of his shoes is preserved in the museum of the Hull Literary and Philosophical Society.

At the west end of Market Weighton Church is a mural tablet, bearing this inscription :—

IN MEMORY OF

WILLIAM BRADLEY,

SON OF JOHN AND MARY BRADLEY,

Of Market Weighton,

WHO DIED 30th MAY, 1820,

AGED 33 YEARS,

He measured 7 feet 9 inches in height and weighed 27 stones.

FOND KIT.

Who, better known in Beverley than Fond Kit, without whom no funeral was complete. When the passenger and mail coaches arrived and departed, there Kit was sure to be, genteel in appearance, with low shoes, carefully tied, blue stockings, knee breeches, light overcoat and soft cap, looking into your face, with a meaningless smile, with his left hand open and extended, and the wrist clasped in his right hand, would repeat his parrot cry, " He' ya a hawp'ny ?" the gift of which would set him bowing and scraping for a long time, and fill his simple heart with childish pleasure. He was not in want, and the halfpence were not spent. No, he would " tak it ti Sally," his sister, with whom he lived. A halfpenny was his desire, and for it he would repeat from

H

memory the tenth chapter of Ninnymiah (Nehemiah), or tell
a tale, which was always short, and about a man " wiv a
heead as soft as a boiled tonnip, an what ran ageean a wall
an smashed it." One thing he was afraid of, and that was
a shilling. To offer him one, was to cause him to run away ;
for a shilling was the emblem of enlistment, and a soldier,
Kit would never be. And thereby hangs a tale. Ask Kit
what made him fond, and he would reply " Rap a tap, tap,
three raps at a barrel." A brighter, smarter boy never lived
than Kit, when he was with his father and mother at the
Fleece Inn, Beckside, Beverley; but, one day, when a
roistering crew of soldiers were billeted there, and the lad
was constantly running into the cellar to bring up frothing
cans of beer for them, one of them, drunker or madder than
the rest, determined to play a practical joke upon him.
Obtaining a white sheet, he went into the dark cellar, while
Kit was temporarily engaged elsewhere, and when the lad
again descended to fill the empty can, he was startled by
three knocks on a barrel. Turning, he beheld this figure in
white, and frightened out of his senses, fled screaming. His
mind was unhinged, and from henceforth he was to be but a
burden, instead of a support; an object of pity, instead of a
source of pride.

He used to ring the death-bell at the Minster, and, with
childish glee, would throw off his coat and pull at the guy
rope, as though the sad sound were music to him, and then
go to the house for cheese and bread, which he looked upon
as his perquisite.

Poor Kit had a mania for old broken teapots and cracked
jars, and after his death, scores of these were found in the
attic of his sister's house, every one of which was crammed
full of the halfpence he had received from the kind-hearted
people who mourned his death, and who felt that their lives
were the poorer, since there had been removed from
their midst, an object of pity, which enabled them to experi-

·ence that it is more blessed to give than to receive. Poor Kit survived his sister, and after her death, he went about saying, "Sally's deead, an Ah's landlady noo."

FOND JIM.

Fond Jim, another half-witted fellow, was contemporaneous with Fond Kit; and Kit would sometimes say "De ya' knaw Jim?" "Yes, Kit, I do! What for?" And Kit would reply, with a pitying smile, " Why, they say he's fond!"

PEG FYFE.

Peg Fyfe was Queen of a robber band, that hesitated not to carry out the most ferocious of her commands. Her name was a terror and a menace throughout East Yorkshire, and many a one was glad to give her whatsover she asked for, for fear of a worse demand from her.

The deed which gave her the distinctive name of "Cruel Peg Fyfe" was perpetrated in Holderness, not far from Spurn Point, where a small farmer cultivated a few acres of land, by the aid of a labourer and a boy. This farmer resisted her exactions as much as possible, but one day, meeting the boy, she told him to leave the stable door open, as she intended stealing the horses. She threatened to skin him alive if he told his master, and such was the terror inspired by her that the lad believed she would do so, if at any future time she had the opportunity. Fear and duty struggled for the mastery, but having determined to do his duty, his Yorkshire wit discovered a way of betraying her intention without speaking to his master. So at night he asked the farmer to come into the stable, and he, wondering, followed, and heard the boy *tell the horses* of Peg's plan, and how sorry he would be in the morning to find them gone, and how harshly they might be treated by the robbers. Though the horses might be no wiser, their master was, and he laid plans to frustrate the evil designs of the thieves, so

that when they did come they might have a different reception
to what they expected.

About midnight, stealthy steps were heard approaching
the stables, and, in response to the boy's whispered enquiry
"Who's there?" the answer "Peg Fyfe!" was given. A gun
was instantly discharged at them, and a cry of pain told
some one had been struck by the shot, but, in the darkness,
all escaped. When morning came, search was made for the
gang, but, though numerous blood stains shewed some one
had been severely wounded, not one of them could be found
in all the country round.

For a long time, the lad lived in constant dread of Peg's
terrible threat, but weeks, and months, and years wore on,
and no news of Peg, so he grew bolder and less fearful, and
ventured farther away from the house; until, one night, he
was startled to see before him, and close to him, the dreaded
form of Peg Fyfe. When he tried to escape, she gave a sign,
and six or seven stalwart men seized him, stripped him,
bound him, and, taking out their knives, proceeded to flay
him alive, while their fiendish leader looked on and taunted
him. Though suffering intense agony, and writhing with
pain, he would allow no groan to escape him, until their
cruel knives took the skin off the palms of his hands and the
soles of his feet, and then he could contain no longer, but
groaned and cried under the terrible pain. When their work
was completed, they left him to find his way home, and his
poor bleeding feet dragged their weary way, painfully home-
ward. All night he was away from home, and troubled
hearts there feared that something had happened to him;
but they never could expect to see such an object as met
their eyes that morning. A faint knock at the door, a weak
cry, and there before them lay a gory mass, in which they
scarcely recognised the poor fellow. He was tenderly taken
up in a sheet, but soon died from the dreadful treatment he
had received.

Vengeance was uppermost in every mind, but, though the country was determinedly scoured, no traces of the murderers could be found, or lynch-law would have been the order of the day.

There is a Gallows Hill between Market Weighton and Shipton, and tradition says that Peg Fyfe was hanged there. It is related that one of her band was hanged on Knavesmire Gallows, and as he was being taken to execution in the cart used for that purpose, his wife called out from the crowd "Ah say, Tom! Hev Ah ti set oor gardin wi taties this back end?" "Ah deeant care what thoo diz," replied Tom. "Deeah what tha likes. D—— it all! Ah nivver was se' mad i' all mi life afooar."

SNOWDON DUNHILL.

At the beginning of the present century, it was dangerous to travel after night-fall in this part of the country, for Snowdon Dunhill and his gang terrorised the district, although highway robbers they were not. In 1813, he was sentenced to seven years transportation for robbing the granary of Mr. Clarkson, of Holme. He served his time, returned to England, and lived for a time in De-la-Pole Court, Manor Street, Hull; but recommencing his old practice was, in 1825, sentenced to transportation for life. The whole family history is such a tissue of crime as to be almost incredible. Snowdon's wife, the widow of a thief, was transported for her crimes. His eldest son, George, was executed in Van Dieman's Land, having been transported from England. Rose, his favourite daughter, cohabited with two men, both of whom were transported, and she was a convict in York Castle. Another daughter, Sarah, was transported, as were also her three husbands. His other son, William, was also transported, but died immediately after his arrival in New South Wales; while Robert Taylor, a son of Mrs. Dunhill's by her former husband, also suffered transportation.

JEREMIAH FOUND.

There once stood in Welton Churchyard, a gravestone bearing the inscription :—

"Here lies Jeremiah Found, who has eight times married been,
  But now old age has caught him in his cage, and he lies under the grass so green."

It is related that one stormy night, when the old sexton, who was a bachelor, was returning home after ringing the death-bell, he stumbled over a bundle, from which issued a muffled cry. Picking up the bundle, he was surprised and dismayed to find therein a child, which he determined to send to the workhouse, but his housekeeper so pleaded for its adoption that he gave way, and by the advice of the clergyman, the babe was christened Jeremiah Found, because he had been *found* by *Jeremiah*. The boy grew, and after much marriage, died at the ripe old age of ninety six.

"BUCKEY" BARNBY.

"Buckey" Barnby, of Malton, was quite a hero in his day.   His nickname was given to him because of his saying "My buck," when speaking to anyone.

One year he engaged himself as waggoner to Mr. John Wilson, Hessle House, and managed to run foul of a gate and smash it.   After harvest, he met Mr. Wilson in the market and had the impudence to say "Diz tha want ony hand yats makkin, mi buck?" On one occasion in the Primitive Methodist Chapel, he kept the collector standing a considerable time, while fumbling for a stray coin, and then said "Noo, mi buck, ah'll o'e tha a penny."

When "three sheets in the wind" which was often, how droll he was.   One night, when in this condition, he was discovered caressing a lamp post, and on being asked what he was doing there, replied "Why, mi buck, Ah's watching

toon ton (turn) roond ; an Ah thowt oor hoose wad be comin'
seean (soon), an then Ah'd pop in."

JIMMY WELBOURN.

Mr. Thos. Holderness writes : "Perhaps the last survivor
of journeyman weavers in Bridlington, was Old Jimmy
Welbourn. Jimmy was a little, thin, wiry, old man, with
knee breeches and ribbed stockings, and wore a very long
frock coat, of primitive cut. He could read, but he could
not write, and was particularly fond of studying a large
illustrated edition of "Cooalpepper Yahbley Beuk" (Culpepper's Herbal). He was a firm believer in astrology.
This made him a skilful disciple of old Culpepper, for he
was always very particular to gather his "yerbs" when
certain planets were in certain positions, as he believed that
unless he did so they would not possess their desired
medicinal properties. Ignorant and superstitious as
the old man was, he must have had remarkable
arithmetical and mathematical abilities, for a friend
once set him the question, 'If a Pope could pray a
soul out of purgatory in an hour, a cardinal in two
hours, an archbishop in three hours, how long would it take
them to do it if they all prayed together?' The old man set
his whole soul on the task, and some time after went to see his
young friend, and said 'Ah've deean it!' His friend looked
at Jimmy's paper and said 'Why, Jimmy, what are all
these?' 'Figures!' answered Jimmy. 'Figures! Do you call
these figures?' 'Yes!' responded Jimmy ; for, being ignorant
of figures, he had invented a set of his own, and with these
nondescript signs had correctly solved the problem."

TOM MOMAN.

Should anyone perform a foolish action, or say a silly
thing, it is probable he might be called "Tom Moman"
in derision, after a half-witted, shrewd character, who was
well known in the northern part of East Yorkshire some

sixty or seventy years ago. He spent one-half of his life in the workhouse, and when not there did odd jobs, such as cattle driving, going errands, &c. Many are the stories told of Tom's knavish tricks, and the relation of one or two will best shew his character. In a certain village, was a mean, miserly man, who delighted in making a bargain, and in over-reaching those who dealt with him. He farmed a small piece of ground, of which part had been set with potatoes, now duly made into a large pie at the top end of the field. One dark night, Tom presented himself at the miser's door, with a heavy sack of potatoes for sale, and, the man knowing he had one of weak intellect to deal with, bantered poor Tom down until sixpence was fixed as the price. On departing, Tom was requested to bring some more at the same price, which, after a moment's thought, he agreed to do. Sack after sack, every few nights, was brought and duly paid for, and the wicked old miser gloated over his ill-gotten gains. Thinking to reward Tom by giving him a little work, he asked him to come and empty the "pie," and wheel all the potatoes into an outhouse. Tom never came, and on the man proceeding to the field, he found the "pie" had been rifled. He had been buying his own potatoes, and this was Tom's revenge on the man for over-reaching him with regard to the first sack, by which Tom had come honestly. Poor Tom was frozen to death in a snowdrift, near Thirkleby, in 1823.

CHAPTER XI

Trees, Plants, and Flowers.

THE universal love of flowers has been the source of almost never-ending lore—flowers at feasts, at weddings, at burials, for use and for ornament. From the Norseman's ash and the Druid's mistletoe there stretch connecting links to our nineteenth century customs. In olden time, witches feared to come near the sacred parasite, but modern witches love its sacred presence, and under its shade bewitching customs are practised.

If an apple remain on the tree until the spring, as it sometimes will, if not gathered, it is considered a sign of death in the family of the owner of the tree. Or if the apple-tree bear blossom and fruit at the same time, a like result would follow; whence the following couplet :—

> " A bloom on the tree, when apples are ripe,
> Is a sure termination of somebody's life."

The latter has been verified (1889) in the case of an old lady in Hull,* in whose garden an apple tree bore a beautiful cluster of blossom at midsummer, when the fruit was growing to maturity.

* See p. 42.

A young woman will endeavour to peel an apple without breaking the peel, and then, throwing it over her left shoulder, will observe what letter is formed, when it has fallen to the ground; such letter being the initial letter of her future husband's name.

Carters put a spray of "esh" (ash) in the head stall of their horses, during summer time, to keep off the flies; but I have also seen it used as an ornament, when flies are not troublesome. The seeds of the ash are termed "kitty-keis."

The flowers of the "humlock" (hemlock) are known as "badman-whotmeal" (oatmeal), a name doubtless given to prevent children playing with the noisome weed. Boys, however, make whistles of its hollow stem.

In digging up "tatics" (potatoes), some are, occasionally, left accidentally in the ground, and these, in the following spring, grow up, but do not give any produce worth taking up. They are called "basthad-taties" (bastard potatoes).

The fragile, blue flowers of the germander speedwell are, with a beautiful sense of fitness, termed "bird eyes;" and children do not like to pluck them for fear the birds will peck their eyes out.

The word "berries" is applied to black, red, and white currants; so that "black berries" are black currants, and not bramble berries.

The elder tree is known as the "bo-ther-y three." Boys remove the pith from the middle of the stem and make pop-guns of the tube thus formed. Formerly, shoemakers made their pegs of the wood, for it is soft and easily worked. The berries are gathered when ripe, and made into jam or wine, both considered efficacious for coughs and colds. The leaves, gathered while the dew is on them, are strewn on the floor of a room infested with fleas, &c., and the pests are killed by sticking to the leaves.

The wild mustard (charlock) is called either "brassock" or "ketlocks." It is believed that the weather, which pro-

duces a good crop of brassocks, is favourable for turnips.
Hence the proverb :—" A brassock year, a tonnap year.

Country children gather the delicate, brittle shoots of the
wild rose, peel off the skin, and eat the soft, juicy wood,
calling it "bread and cheese." Hawthorn leaves bear the
same name.

The wild plum is called "bullace ;" and the brightness of
its skin has given rise to the simile :—" As breet (bright) as
a bullace."

" Burr " is the name given to the prickly seed-case of the
chestnut ; also to the round, hairy seed-cases of the goose-
grass. As these cases catch and stick to the things that
touch them, it has given rise to a saying " It sticks like a
burr." The goose-grass has many names : hairiff, hairup,
catchweed, cleaver, fat-hen, tongue-bleeder ; but children,
when they see a piece of it sticking to your dress, say you
have got a sweetheart.

When children find a flower of the celandine or buttercup,
they pluck it, hold it under the smooth, fair chin of their
comrades, to see "if they like butter." The liking is proportional to the brightness of the yellow reflection on the
skin.

The flowers of the hawthorn are called " May " from the
time when it used to flower ; and the scarlet berries, which
follow, are " cat-haws." Is it humour, which has designated
the red hips of the wild rose, " dog-chowps," from the cat and
dog life which they lead, tearing each other in the hedgerow ?
The wild rose itself is termed the dog rose ; and we have
also dog-daisy, the common daisy as distinguished from the
large ox-eye daisy (Marguerites, according to fashion) ; and
dog-oak, as distinguished from the oak tree, the royal oak.

Children will not gather or smell at the beautiful yellow
flower of the dandelion, " piss-a-bed " or " pissimire " they
call it, because they believe unpleasant results, as recorded
in the former name, will ensue. The leaves of the plant

grow close to the ground, but the flower stalk grows erect, though hollow and easily broken. As a conceited person walks with head erect, it is said "He walks as brant (upright) as a pissimire."

Children, however, delight to pluck the flower stalks, when the fluffy ball of downy seeds is quite ripe. They call them "clocks," and puff at them, scattering the winged seeds broadcast. The number of puffs required to dislodge the whole, denotes the time of day, and the little rogues regulate the length and strength of the puffs, on purpose to bring matters right, believing it best to prophesy only when you know.

> " Dandelion, with globe of down,
> The school-boy's clock in every town,
> Which the truant puffs amain,
> To conjure lost hours back again."

When a four-leaved clover is found, it ought to be placed in the heel of your left boot, then, the first person you meet of the opposite sex is to be your life partner. I am told this is infallible. A Devonshire saying is :—

> " An even-leaved ash,
> And a four-leaved clover,
> You 'll see your true love
> 'Fore the day is over."

The scarlet poppy, which makes our corn-fields so brilliant, is named the "heead-wahk" (head-ache), because it will give you head-ache either to smell or look long at it.

The "hoos-lock" (house-leek) is grown largely on the roofs of houses, thatched ones especially, as a preventive against fire.

The long strong leaves of the iris are called "swords" by children, and are used as such when they play at soldiers.

The bright yellow flower of the " whin " (furze, gorse) can be gathered nearly all the year round. Hence the saying, " Kissing is out of fashion when the whin is out of bloom." Long, narrow faggots, termed " whin-kids," are used to form helms (shelters) for cattle in fields. To form these " whin-kids " the " whin-busks " (bushes) are cut down, tied in narrow bundles and then fastened to the wooden framework of the intended shelter.

Docken or Dockin is the name given to the common dock-weed, which is used as an antidote to the sting of a nettle. Children rub the part, saying,—

> " Nettle oot,
> Dockin in."

Children impose on one another by saying " Nettles won't sting to-day " and grasp it firmly unhurt to support their assertion, while their timorous unbelieving comrade scarcely touches it, and is stung for his want of firmness. The young tender shoots of the nettle are gathered in spring, and used as a vegetable for dinner.

The sorrel is known as " soor-dockin " or " green sauce " and is gathered by children and eaten, though they believe it grows only where dead men have been.

Lin (flax) used to be largely grown in Holderness but it is like hand-loom weaving and whale fishing, a departed industry. From lin, a coarse, linen material, called " harden," was made. The seed of the lin is linseed, and the product of its manufacture, linen.

The rowan, or mountain ash is prized because of the protection it affords against witches. Carters like a whip-stock of it, for,

> " If you're whip-stock's made of rowan,
> You may gan through ony toon."

Respecting its power over witches, the Rev. H. E. Maddock,

M.A., Patrington, told me the following. In the late autumn of 1889, an old woman in Patrington came to Mrs. Maddock, asking for a piece of the rowan tree, which stood in the vicarage grounds. Ever obliging, Mrs. Maddock consented, adding "Do not take many of the berries." The woman then said she did not want the berries, but a piece of the wood. Further enquiries elicited the information that it was wanted to make a cross, and when the old woman felt unwell (of course, due to the malevolence of some witch) she spoke to this cross, and it made her better. The wood was to be gathered at mid-day; but, as an additional request, the old woman said "If this does not answer, will you let my son come at midnight to get some more." This midnight gathering evidently was believed to be more efficacious.

The wych elm, known as witch elm, is believed to be so called because witches dread it, so country carters put a sprig on their horses, and carry a piece of wood in their own pockets.

The wild apple, ever keenly sour, is called a "crab," and its sourness is proverbial—"As soor as a crab."

A cabbage in the dialect is a "cabbish;" and, when anyone assumes innocence or ignorance, it is said "He's as green as a yalla cabbish (yellow cabbage)."

The spear grass is used by boys in divining their future occupation. Beginning at the bottom spikelet, they pick off one for each word they say of the following, and the word which falls to the last spikelet will be their future trade or profession.

> " Tinker, tailor,
> Soldier, sailor,
> Rich man, poor man,
> Beggar man, thief."

The blackness of the sloe has given rise to the well known proverb—"As black as a sloe."

A piece of seaweed is frequently hung up behind the door, and its condition is indicative of the weather. If it grow damp, rain may be expected ; if it remain dry, then the weather will be fine.

In the carrs, or lowlands, of Holderness, there are often turned up huge trunks, stumps, and roots of immense trees, black as coal. When the men are ploughing, they carry a bundle of sticks, and when the plough strikes against one of these buried trees, the ploughman leaves one of his sticks upright in the ground. After the work is finished, attention is then paid to these timbers, sometimes 80 or 90 feet long and so firmly embedded that they are blasted with gunpowder. They make splendid gate posts, and will easily tear into rails ; and they work to the surface in such quantities that if a field be left unploughed for a year or two, it is almost impossible to plough it. Six hundred trees were taken out of a 14 acre field in Routh Carrs, in 1838. The prevalent belief is that all these trees were brought down by the Flood, and the common name for the wood is Awd Nooah (Old Noah).

A kind of fungus is called a toad stool, and children are told not to gather them because toads have sat thereon ; and both toads and newts are considered venomous and hurtful.

The dark green rings, common in old pastures, are " fairy rings," because here the fairies sport and play, dancing round their Queen.

It is believed to be unlucky to gather all fruit off the tree ; so a few deformed apples, pears, or berries, are left hanging for the birds, it is said, but do not the birds here stand for the fairies ?

The following are the names of plants &c. in the folk speech of East Yorkshire :—Brammle (bramble), bulls and coos (cuckoo pint), cat tails (common bulrush), daffy-down-dilly (daffodil), damsil (damson plums), fog (after math, grass after hay), foal-foot (colts' foot), hezzle (hazel), hoss gogs (wild plums), hoss knops (knap weed), ladies fingers (crow feet), laylock (lilac), lintins or tars (tares), London pride (Sweet William; never the plant popularly so called), Nancy pretty (London pride), owm (elm), paums (palms), prick hollan (holly), semper, rock semper (samphire), salary (celery), seggy (sycamore), sparra grass (asparagas), thrimlin jockies (quaking grass), wicks (couch grass), wilf (willow), yak (oak), tars (tares).

CHAPTER XII.

𝕭irds, 𝕬nimals, 𝕵nsects.

BIRDS.

TO a country man, birds are a constant presence, and though fewer are found in towns, it is probable there are more than people think. I have a small garden in Hull, almost surrounded by houses, yet therein, I have either seen or heard thirty-three different kinds of birds, including the night hawk (night jar) and the heron.

Among birds, the robin, both in England and France, is accounted sacred by boys, who will not rob its nest of eggs or young ones. Should a boy do so, his companions hoot and hiss at him, singing all the while :—

> " Robbin takker, robbin takker,
>   Sin, sin, sin ! "

until he be driven from their midst.

It is believed that, in the autumn, the young robins hunt and kill the old ones,

Should this bird go about the hedge chirping mournfully, though the day be bright and the sky cloudless, it will rain ere long; and when you see him singing cheerfully, on some topmost twig, it will soon be fine, though the rain be pouring down.

It is believed that if anyone kill a robin, some dire calamity will happen to the family of the slayer. When boys are hunting birds in winter, and the poor little things are bewildered by stones and shouts, all sport will suddenly cease, if it be discovered that the bird is a robin, and the creature allowed to escape.

If pigeons congregate on the ridge of the house roof it foretells a storm of wind or rain; while the presence of pigeon's feathers in a bed makes it very hard for anyone to die thereon. White pigeons alighting on a house or near to a person is a sign of death. The stockdove, so called from its nesting in the *stocks* of trees, is locally known as a "stoggie."

The common cock is believed to have foreknowledge of the coming of unexpected visitors, or of death; and to give intimation by crowing. Said a friend to me, "I'm sure somebody must be coming to our house, for our cock came to the kitchen door and crowed three times." In fact, a sister did call unexpectedly, and so belief in the cock as a prophet was strengthened. The *Holderness Glossary* relates a story of an old farmer, who was trying to convince an unbelieving friend that cocks could foretell events, and, addressing the sceptic, said, "Diz thoo meean ti tell me, at oor awd cock dizzn't knaw when there's boon ti be a deeath iv oor family?" When a person is very certain about any thing, he is said to be "cock-sure;" and he who is conceited because of his certain knowledge is "cocky."

The land-rail is termed the corn-crake, from its frequenting corn fields, and from its harsh cry. The frequent calling of this bird is said to be indicative of rain.

Children, in Germany as well as in England, listen for the cry of the cockoo, after saying :—

> " Cuckoo, cherry tree,
> Come down, tell me,
> How many years I have to live."

and they believe the years will be the number of cries given by the bird. A rhyme, relative to the time of her sojourn, runs thus :—

> " Cuckoo in April,
> Cuckoo in May,
> Cuckoo in June,
> Then she flies away."

It is fortunate if you have money in your pocket when you first hear the cuckoo in any year. If you turn it then, you will have money in your purse until the cuckoo comes again. From the hawk-like flight of the bird, it is believed that cuckoos turn into hawks during the winter. Its frequent calling is a sign of rain ; and before the bird emigrates, its call is less full and more indistinct, sometimes failing to give utterance to one distinct "cuckoo." Hence the saying, " Cuckoo 'll seean be gannin ; she chatters rarely."

It is considered lucky for swallows to build their nests under the eaves of your house, and dire results will follow if the nests be disturbed, or are forsaken by the birds. Henderson (p. 122) says :—"A farmer's wife, near Hull, told a friend of mine, how some young men, sons of a banker in that town, had pulled down all the swallows' nests about a little farm, which their father possessed. 'The bank broke soon after,' she said, 'and, poor things, the family have had naught but trouble since.'" This notion of ill-luck following the disturbance of birds' nests, is not confined to the swallow. In the spring of 1886, a rook built its nest in the solitary tree standing in the yard of Mr. Cass, Prospect Street, Hull, and when any mischievous lads came to molest it, an old lady in Portland Street used to drive them away with her sweeping brush; for had the rook been compelled to forsake its nest, the whole neighbourhood would have participated in the consequent ill-luck.

A common couplet respecting the crow is used both in Lancashire and Yorkshire :—

> "Crow, crow, get out o' my sight,
> Or else I'll eat your liver and lights."

Rooks are termed "craws," and crows are "greybacks," "Garton greybacks," or "Wetwang greybacks" from their favourite haunts. If rooks suddenly leave their rookery, misfortune may be looked for. As rooks fly straight from roosting place to feeding ground, it has given rise to the proverb, "as the crow flies." And it is said that if you do not wear something new at Easter, rooks will spoil your clothes.

The storms, which occur in spring and autumn, about the time of arrival and departure of the swallow, are known as "swallow storms."

The bittern, known as the "butther bump" is now a *rara avis* in this district, but the following couplet preserves its name :—

> "When the butther bumps cry,
> Summer is nigh."

The frequent cry of the peacock is indicative of rain.

> "When the peacock loudly calls,
> Then look out for rain and squalls."

Though peacock feathers are now fashionable and æsthetic, they are looked upon with disfavour by those of the old school, for these feathers were always deemed unlucky. Some æsthetic friends, in choosing a "fairing," selected a lovely fire-screen, made of peacock's feathers. The person to whom it was sent was greatly troubled about it, and, after spending several days in great mental distress, actually burnt the costly gift, being fearful of the ill-luck its possession would entail.

The following are dialect names connected with birds :— Golly, gollin, gollock (an unfledged bird), banty cock (bantam cock), cletch (a brood), herrin sue (heron), stahnil (starling), steg (gander), willy-wagtail (wagtail), jinny oolat (owl), billy biter (blue titmouse), charley cock (missel thrush), thrushie (thrush), blackie (blackbird), felfar (field fare), fire-tail (red start), peggy chatter (whitethroat), nettle monger (black cap), feather poke (long-tailed titmouse), cuddie (hedge sparrow), tom tit (wren), redcap (gold finch), green linnet (green finch), spadger (sparrow), weetie or bull spink (chaffinch), goldie (yellow hammer), maggie or nanpie (magpie), peewit or teeafit (lapwing), yaffler (green woodpecker), kitty ake (kittiwake), scoot (common guillemot), parrot (razor bill).

ANIMALS.

Of animals, the weasel is known as the "rezzil," and its wakefulness and quickness have caused the proverbs, "As shahp as a rezzil ;" and "Catch a weasel asleep if you can."

The snail, because of its slow motion, has given rise to the derisive expression, "a sneel gallop." When children find a snail, they say to it :

" Sneel, sneel, put oot yer horn,
   Or else Ah'll kill yer fayther and muther ti-morn."

The hedgehog is known as the "pricky back otchun" (urchin), and war to the death is declared against it by farmers' men, who say it sucks the teats of the cows as they lie in the pastures, and so reduces the yield of milk.

Of bovine names, the calf is a "cauf," or "moddie cauf;" and when a child's hair has an inclination to stand upright, or incline backward from the forehead, it is said to be "cauf-licked," doubtless from its similarity to the hair of the calf after it has been licked by the cow. A young bullock is a "stot," and a young heifer, a "whye." It is scarcely fifty years ago since oxen were used as beasts of burden, in farming operations.* They are still used in the south of England and on the continent, but are never seen now in East Yorkshire. An aged farmer said to me " Ah've seen oxen gie way ti hosses, and noo hosses hez ti gi' way ti steeam ploos." When a waggon stuck fast on a bad road, it was once a regular custom to unyoke the horses, fetch the old bull and five-year-old steer, give the bull the hardest corner, and then, with a long pull, a strong pull, and a pull all together, the waggon was righted, if the gearing held.

Other animal names are :—club start (a kind of pole cat), fooamad or fummat (polecat), fuzzack (donkey), moudie, or moudwarp (mole). Saying respecting some of these: "It stinks like a fummat ;" "As blind as a mole."

The marks on the neck and back of the donkey form a cross, indicative of the entry into Jerusalem.

Among the Flambro' fishermen it is reckoned a most unlucky thing to speak about a pig while baiting their lines; and still more so to see one, when going fishing. "Ay, " said an old fisherman to me, " If Ah said owt aboot a pig, whahle we were baiting lines i' mi uncle shade (shed), oot Ah had ti gooa, an that shahp."

The hare is a most unlucky animal to meet. If you can only get straight in front of one, it will almost run against you. One man told me that a hare had actually run between his legs, as he stood motionless, transfixed with terror at the thought of the evil which must befall him at such a catastrophe. Visits, and even weddings, have been postponed, because a hare crossed the path. When a person acts wildly and strangely, he is said to be "as mad as a March hare."

* T. Bainton, Esq., Arram Hall, informs me oxen were used by them until 1845, and that they still possess the yokes, which, by his kind permission, I have seen.

The badger is believed to have the two legs on the one side shorter than those on the other side, as well as having the two fore legs shorter than the two hinder ones, thus enabling the animal to run quickest and best across and up a hill side.

On the 21st September, the common saying relative to the weather is, " If the buck rises with a dry horn, we shall have a Michaelmas summer."

If any one be bitten by a dog, it is believed that if at any future time the dog goes mad, the person bitten will also do so. To prevent this, the dog must be killed. Dr. R. Wood, Driffield, relates how a man came to him suffering from a severe bite in the upper arm, given by a large dog. The wound soon healed, but the man grew so low-spirited at the fate which might be his, so long as the dog lived, that, in in the end, the dog was destroyed. The howling of a dog portends death.

When horses stand with their backs to the hedge, or the cat sits with her back to the fire, a storm may be expected.

As the bats flit about in the twilight, children, throwing up their caps for the creature to come under, say :—

> " Black, black boear-a-way,
> Cum doon bi here a-way !"

Another name for the bat is " flitter-mouse ;" and its apparently aimless flight is suggestive of blindness; hence the proverb, " As blinnd as a bat."

It is considered lucky to have a black cat, but unlucky to meet one. Henderson (p. 171) says that a few years ago, in Scarborough, sailors' wives were in the habit of keeping a black cat, to ensure the safety of their husbands at sea. If a cat sneeze, it is believed that the disease will be taken by all in the house, so when it does sneeze, the cat is quickly turned out, to prevent, in some degree, the threatened epidemic.

Earth worms that have been cut in pieces are believed to grow into as many worms as there are pieces.

INSECTS.

When bees swarm, if they alight on a dead branch, it is a sign of death in the family ; and such calamity will occur within a twelvemonth. At a death, it used to be customary to tie a piece of crape round the bee-hives, and give the bees a funeral biscuit. This neglected, trouble and loss would surely follow. To kill a bee will surely cause ill-fortune.

The little round-bodied spider is termed a "money spider," from the belief that its presence brings good fortune. I have seen boys hold their hands in its way, and struggle for the best place, so that the little creature may run on them, and so bring luck. To kill one is to court misfortune. A couplet says : —

" He who would wish to thrive,
  Must let spiders run alive."

One fine day in August, 1889, I was watching some boys amusing themselves with kicking a small ball about. In the midst of a scrimmage, the game was suddenly arrested by a loud cry of "Stop!" and while the players stood watching, one of them stooped down, picked up a small bright-backed beetle, and carried it off to a place of safety, saying as he did so, "I don't want it to rain to-day." He had picked up a "rain-clock," which is never killed by children, or else it will rain.

Should the earwig get into your ear, it will eat its way to the brain and kill you. It is called a "forkin robin," or " battle twig."

The white, frothy exudation from the brock is known as "frog spit," and is believed to be poisonous. A common saying is, "Ah sweeats like a brock."

When children find a lady-bird, or cushy-cow-lady, they say,

> " Lady bird, lady bird, fly away home,
> Your house is on fire, and your children all gone."

The little insect which makes a ticking sound at the head of a bed is called the "death watch," and is popularly supposed to notify death.

It is considered lucky to have crickets in the house, and unlucky to kill one ; and if you put one in the fire it will not burn.

Among other insect names are, Tommy Taylor, or Daddy long legs (crane fly), cleg, or gleg (gadfly), lop (flea), mawk (maggot), midge (gnat), clocks, or black clocks (black beetles).

CHAPTER XIII.

𝕷𝖊𝖊𝖈𝖍𝖈𝖗𝖆𝖋𝖙.

" 'Throw physic to the dogs; I'll none of it."
Macbeth, v., 3.

TO ease pain, man will try almost every suggested remedy, and when he has tried numberless things, each of which was alleged to be a certain cure, he reverts to some simple thing, taught him by his old grandmother, and which, because of its simplicity, he had at first contemptuously rejected, in favour of more complex but inefficacious compounds.

John Wesley, in his *Primitive Physic*, advises boiled carrots for asthma, a decoction of boxwood for baldness, the juice of nettles for blood-spitting, goose-grass for cancer, and six middling cobwebs for ague. In his day (says the *Hospital*), nothing but tradition, practice, and shrewd observation led him to extol these native remedies. It is only of late that chemists have found that the carrot, when wild, possesses a volatile principle, which stimulates the bronchial membrane and promotes expectoration; that the box-tree furnishes buxine, which specially excites the nerves of the hair bulbs; that the stinging hairs of the nettle are endowed with formic acid, which serves to arrest bleeding; that goose-grass is rich in tannin for the relief of cancerous sores ; and that the spider's web exercises a particular virtue against ague, because of its containing a medical substance analagous to quinine.

Among natural poultices, cow's dung holds a foremost place. It is a sovereign remedy, especially if fresh, for scalds, burns, bad breasts, and all kinds of sores. Dr. R. Wood, Driffield, has seen it used for a bad breast, and has had to order its removal before the necessary examination could be made.

An aged man told me how he was cured of a bunion. When a boy, he was hobbling about the house, using the sweeping-brush as a crutch. A neighbour, coming in, asked what was the matter, and on being told, said, " Oh ! get some coo clap (cow dung), mix it wi' fish oil (whale oil), put it on, and let it stop on all neet." He did so, but never slept all the night for pain. Neither next day, nor since, has he had any trouble with it, and "that's sixty year sin" he added.

A man, whose right hand and fore-arm were covered with sores, used to attend at the Hull shambles, on "killing days," and when an animal was slaughtered, the butcher cut a slit in the stomach of the newly killed animal. Into this, the man thrust his hand and arm, and kept it there, until the contents of the stomach cooled down. A few applications healed the part. Infants also have thus been inserted, when largely covered with sores.

The milt, or soft roe of a fish, is used for "gathered" (inflamed) fingers. The milt is opened, the finger placed therein, the whole bound on, and it is not removed, except under compulsion from the offensive odour, or that the need of it is no longer felt.

The following sickening remedy for a swollen knee has recently been used in veterinary practice, but it was considered efficacious, and used with effect, on the human frame. Kill a cat, split the body length-wise, and apply it while warm to

the knee, bind it thereon, and there let it stay, until the cure
is complete.   A fowl answers quite as well.

A poultice made of rotten apples is often used for
weak eyes, and for "botches" (small boils).   Apples, good, ripe
and raw, are used as a corrective medicine, justifying the
modern maxim,

> "To eat an apple going to bed,
> The doctor then will beg his bread."

Sheep's dung is applied in a poultice, for the cure of
erysipelas : and the same material boiled with new milk,
until fully dissolved, is taken internally for the removal and
prevention of gall-stones.   Dog's dung, under the disguise of
Album Græcum, formed an important item in the old
formulas, and goose dung is a common remedy for baldness,
while human urine is commonly used for chapped hands.
Cow's urine is in demand for scald head, but ox-gall is often
used for the same complaint.

A certain fungus, which grows in the fields, is known as
"puff-ball," and often grows to a considerable size.   When
ripe, it is filled with a soft, brown, powdery substance, which
is commonly and successfully used to stop bleeding from
wounds.   The material is spread over the wound and bound
on, just as tobacco is used for the same purpose.   Salt also
is scattered on slight cuts to take away the soreness as well
as to stop the flow of blood.   Though to stop bleeding at the
nose, a cold door key is put down the patient's back, or a
cloth dipped in cold water is applied to the nape of the neck,
or, as a last resource, a little roll of white paper is kept under
the tongue.

To cure the king-cough, or whooping cough, procure, if
possible, a hairy worm, *i.e.*, the hairy caterpillar of certain
butterflies, and suspend it in a flannel cover round the neck
of the sufferer.   As the creature dies and wastes away, so
will the cough depart.

For the cure of warts, a grey snail is necessary. Rub the slimy creature on the warts, and afterwards impale the poor thing on a thorn. Result—disappearance of both. But for those who, under pretence of necessity, would like to indulge their predatory proclivities, it is necessary to steal a piece of beef, rub the warts with the ill-gotten flesh, and then bury the beef. This stealing and rubbing establishes such an affinity, that the one dies as the other decays.

Is it because an ass carried our Lord that the same animal is used to charm and carry away whooping cough? Children suffering therefrom are passed twice or thrice under the belly of the animal, in the belief that such a strange, stupid piece of work will effect a cure. Additional efficacy is secured by giving the child to eat two or three hairs of the donkey, between two slices of bread and butter.

A startling remedy for thrush, but one considered highly beneficial, is to catch a frog, place it in a muslin bag, and give it to the infant to suck.

In Leechcraft, the moon exercised an important influence, both in the gathering of herbs, and in performing operations. Best (p. 23.) says :—"The usuall and best time for geldinge of lambs is aboute the middle or 20th of June, the moone beinge four or six dayes past the full."

Old almanacks have a column in which parts of the body —head, arms, loins, &c.—are placed opposite the days of the month; and no operation was performed on any part of the body except on the day specially favourable, according to this table. No one would have his hair cut except on a day which had the word "head" opposite to it; but even then superstition might prevent it, if Friday were the day, for :—

" Friday hair,
Sunday horn,
You'll go to devil
Afore Monday morn."

So that ill-luck will follow the cutting of hair on a Friday, or the trimming of nails on a Sunday.

Dr. R. Wood was once sitting with an old farmer, engaged in conversation, when the sitting-room door opened, and the farmer's son, half entering, asked "Shall we geld them lambs ti moan, fayther?" "Why! Ah decant knaw! What's almanack say?" The oracle was consulted, and declared against the proposed day, for the proper part was not opposite the morrow. The operation was postponed, and another day was fixed in accordance with the arrangement in the almanack.

Herbs were considered to be beneficial for the relief of such ailments as those to which they were supposed to bear the most resemblance, either in colour or shape; as yellow Turkey rhubarb for bile, lichen or liverwort for complaints of the liver. Apparently on the same principle a glass of vinegar is still given to a drunken man to sober him, and Egyptian ladies used the blood of a black calf or bull, mixed with oil, as a hair dye and restorative.

Among diet cures, snails, as food, are taken to cure consumption; a roasted mouse for croup; a mouse pie for incontinence of urine; rat pie for whooping cough, and live slugs for asthma, the slugs to be swallowed like oysters.

The smoke from a burning limekiln is considered good for bronchial affections, and I have seen mothers leading their little ones to and fro through the smoke, until the poor little things were nearly stifled.

May dew, gathered at sunrise, is used as a preservative, rendering the skin permanently soft and velvety; this dew, snuffed up the nostrils, will cure vertigo.

By carrying a potatoe in the pocket, rheumatism may be cured, and as it grows black and withers, the disease will depart. Not many weeks ago, a man wished to shew me some antiquity he had found, but his jacket pocket was so filled with odds and ends ("kelterment," he called it), that he turned all out in order to better prosecute his search. Among the miscellaneous collection I noticed a potato, withered, dry, hard and black, and was informed it was kept as a preventive and cure for rheumatism.

Herbs enter largely into Folk Medicine, and in order to preserve their full virtues, it is necessary to gather them at certain stages of the moon, or at some particular hour of the day or night, either mid-day or mid-night, the latter being more efficacious. Best (p. 164), gives a cure for worms in children —"Take worm-wood, rue, bull's gall and hog's grease; fry all together; apply to the child's navel, and anoint the stomach with the same."

If infants be troubled with flatulence, a small quantity of water is put into a cup, and a red-hot cinder is dropped into the water, which is then given to relieve the little sufferer. Or a decoction of carraway seeds is given which is called "dill-water." *

Many people make wine and jelly from elder-berries, or from black currants, and this wine or jelly is used to ameliorate affections of the throat. A dame of the old school would condemn the making of black currant jam as wasteful, and a misuse of the good things of nature, in using a medicine as food.

Fuller's earth, powered, is used for soreness and inflammation; shoemaker's wax, as an ointment for boils; goose fat as an emollient, both for the human skin and leathern articles; and treacle as an ointment for rheumatic swellings.

Tar, soot, powdered shells, calcined flints, wood ashes, and many other strange articles have all occupied places in the list of remedies used by our ancestors; and the use of some of them is not obsolete yet.

* Dill—Ice. dilla, to lull; to soothe.

CHAPTER XIV.

Games and Sports.

THE common game of "tig" (touch) is, without doubt, a boyish imitation and adaptation of a ceremony performed by our forefathers, long years ago. Yorkshire is divided into wapentakes, and when, in ancient times, a new governor was installed, all freemen were required to come and touch his spear with theirs, as a token of fealty. He who did not do this, became an outlaw.

Boys, in playing at "tig" have a central position, called "home," which, at the installation, would be the chieftain's spear. A leader, called "tig," is chosen, and then all the players run away, crying,

> "Tiggery, tiggery, touch wood,
> You can't catch me!"

The leader pursues, and if he can "tig" a player before that player reaches "home" and touches wood, then the one who has been "tug" becomes the leader, and so on. Touching wood exempts from pursuit. If a player hurt himself, or wish to make any explanation, he can free himself by crying "Kings!" Just as when a King's thane came to the weapon-touching, he would claim exemption by saying that his fealty was paid direct to the king.

There are several variations of this game, one notably called "lame-tig," in which the player must keep one hand on the place where he was touched; the object of the toucher being to touch in as awkward a place as possible.

Another form is "neet-tig," (night-tig) in which each player strives to touch another last, when separating for the night, the victor shouting out "Ah tug yo' last!"

"Cross-tig" is played without a "home," and so is "lame-tig," but in "cross-tig" the toucher must pursue the player, who "crosses," that is, runs across the line of pursuit, between him and his prey. Thus, the toucher is being baulked continually, and the pursued one constantly changing.

"Taws" (marbles) form endless sport, from which neither wet, cold, dirt, nor fear, can drive the eager players. Boys will sometimes play for "nowts" in which no "taws" change hands; but they most frequently play for "good," or for "keepins," when each player takes all he wins.

In "ring taw" a large circle is drawn on the ground, within which the players each place the same number of marbles. They then fix a place some ten or twelve feet distant from the circle, and bowl a large marble to it. The one who gets nearest goes first, and the others in order of nearness, but if a bowling marble enter the circle, it is dead, and the bowler must take the last turn. The first player now shoots his marble at the full ring, and all those he drives out are his; and he can continue shooting until he fails to drive any out, or his own stays in, and then the next in order follows, and so on, until the ring be empty.

A quieter indoor game with marbles is called "eggs in a bush." A boy takes a number of marbles and shakes them in his hands, asking, "How many eggs in a bush?" The one who guesses must pay the difference between the number he

K

says and the actual number, afterwards taking his turn at shaking and asking; but, if he guess correctly, all are his. A similar game is "odds and evens," a few being held in one hand, which is kept closed. If odds be guessed, and there be evens, the guesser gives one; but if odds be guessed, and there be odds, then they become the property of the guesser.

A very popular game is "Hiry hag" or "Haggary hag." A leader having been chosen, he starts from "home," and with his hands clasped, pursues the players, who run away, shouting,

"Haggary hag,
Put him in a bag,
And shak (shake) him up for sawdust."

In some places, they say,

"Hiry, hiry, hag,
Put him in a bag," etc.,

When he "tigs" any one, he unclasps his hands, and both race "home," for if the other players capture them, they must give their captor a ride home. These two, taking hold of hands, the leader or "tigger" with his right hand free, and the other, the catcher, with his left free, pursue the other players, to catch and touch them. When one is touched, then comes the race or ride home, and these three then form a chain, and the game is continued until all are caught and incorporated into one long chain. If, at any time, the chain becomes broken, and the outside players strive to break it, no one can be touched until the chain has been re-formed at "home."

Should a boy be detected in cheating, or in committing an offence against the boys' unwritten law, the discoverer would cry out "Ringlins! Up!" when all within hearing would rush up, and, seizing the unfortunate culprit by the hair, lug (tug, pull) right merrily, until the leader cried, "off!" During the time of the punishment, each one must hum, and he who

did not pull hard enough, or who did too much by not
ceasing when the signal was given, was treated to the same ;
and so the fun ran on, until all had been "ringled" or the
players had grown tired.

Girls play at "Fox and Hen." One is chosen to be the
fox, another to be the hen, and all the rest are the chickens.
The chickens, in Indian file, take hold of each other's waists,
the first one taking hold of the hen's waist. They then go
for a walk, and soon see the fox, when the following
dialogue ensues :—

> *Hen.* "What are you doing?"
> *Fox.* "Picking up sticks."
> *Hen.* "What for?"
> *Fox.* "To make a fire."
> *Hen.* "What's the fire for?"
> *Fox.* "To boil some water."
> *Hen.* "What's the water for?"
> *Fox.* "To boil some chickens in."
> *Hen.* "Where do you get them from?"
> *Fox.* "From you."
> *Hen.* "No! that you won't."

The fox then tries to get hold of the chickens, but the hen
faces the enemy, while her chickens form a line behind her,
to prevent being caught. Should the fox succeed in catching
one, that one becomes the fox, and the fox takes the place of
the hen, and so the game proceeds.

In another outdoor game, girls form a ring, with one of
their number in the centre. As they circle round her,
they sing :—

> "Poor Mary sat a-weeping,
>   A-weeping, a-weeping!
> Poor Mary sat a-weeping,
>   On a fine summer day.
> On the carpet she shall kneel,
>   (*Centre one kneeling, and in attitude of weeping*)
> Till the grass grows in the field.

> Stand up, stand up, upon your feet,   *(Stands)*
> And choose the one, you love so sweet.   *(Chooses one.)*
> And now you're married, I wish you joy,
>   *(Two standing arm in arm)*
> Every year a girl or a boy.
> If one won't do, I wish you two,
> So pray come cuddle and kiss together." *(Kiss)*

The original Mary then joins the circle, leaving the one she has chosen to be Mary the second.

After candle-light, one of the games played round the fire is called "Jack's alive!" A piece of stick is thrust into the fire, until well alight, then withdrawn, and the flame blown out. It is then whirled round quickly by the first player, who hands it to the next, saying, "Jack's alive!" It is passed quickly from one to the other, for whoever holds it when the last spark dies out has to pay a forfeit.

When sitting round the fire, on a winter evening, it used to amuse us to throw pieces of paper therein, and then watch the bright sparks race across the ashes. We used to call them "Folks leaving church," and the names of local characters were given to them as the peculiarity of motion suggested.

Another indoor game was that in which, when one of the party had gone into another room, a name of some animal, bird, fish, &c., was chosen by each one present. The absent one was then recalled, and having the others arranged semicircularly, was asked :—

> " Of all the birds in the air,
>   And the fishes in the sea,
>   Find me a ———— "
>   *(Saying the name chosen by one of the players).*

Each face was then eagerly scanned, and the one betraying consciousness was sure to be selected. If the right one were chosen, that one became the guesser, and a fresh selection of names was made; but if the wrong one were chosen, guess after guess was made until success was secured. Each failure caused much merriment.

In spring time, boys take wild birds' eggs, and having placed some on the ground, a few inches apart, they retire several yards, and try to break the eggs by walking to them blindfolded, and striking with a switch. "Switch egg" they call it.

Another boy's game is played by three boys. One stands upright against a wall, another bends down with his head against the stomach of the first, while the third leaps on to the back thus formed, and holding up so many fingers, speaks to the one on whose back he is,

> "Buck, buck,
> Hoo mony fingers div I hod up?"

"Buck" answers as many as he thinks, say four. If this were wrong, it would be said

> "Fower thoo says,
> An' three there is,
> So buck, buck &c."

until the correct number is guessed.

In another game, called "long-back," sides are chosen, and lots having been cast to determine who shall "set the first back," the losers of the toss form one long back, by joining end on. The other side then leap on, and if the long back be not strong enough to bear the weight, they must "set back" again. If they bear the pressure, then a change is made, and the leapers become the back, and so on.

Cock-fighting, bull-baiting, badger-baiting and such like sports and pastimes are obsolete. Sancton still has its cock-pit, and so has Lund. In the latter village, it is a slight depression, surrounded by trees, not far from the cross on the village green. When anyone says they have been to Lund, it is a test question to ask, "Did you see the cock-pit?" At Driffield, the hollow on the north side of the Moot Hill was used for cock-fighting ; while, at Beverley, the sport was indulged in among the pits in the Newbegin Bushes. In towns, nearly every public-house had its cock-pit; and when a match was arranged, the bellman used to perambulate the streets, giving notice of it. Thus, at Beverley, his cry was, "Cocking to-night, at eight, at the Bay Horse, Lairgate."

In that part of the Beverley Westwood known as the Newbegin Bushes bull-baiting also was practised. Here may still be seen, fastened to a stone sunk in the ground, the identical iron ring to which the bulls were tethered. A similar ring is at Kilham. Opposite the Old Hall, Hornsea, is a triangular-shaped piece of ground called the Bull Ring, the site of the very ring being occupied by a young elm tree, surrounded by an iron guard.

CHAPTER XV.

Nursery Rhymes and Jingles.

TO the seeker after knowledge, nothing is too low or mean for investigation, and to the folk-lorist there are precious particles even in such common-place things as nursery rhymes, and the nonsensical, jangling jingles which are the special delight of young folks. Rhymes are attractive to the ear, so world-wide stories and incidents are strung together in rhymes, and little lips lisp the numbers, and gain ideas and an increased vocabulary in the easiest way.

The following rhymes and jingles are neither inclusive nor exclusive. They do not include all in use in East Yorkshire, neither do they exclude those common to all the country, if they be used locally.

In order to amuse and please the child, the nurse places the infant on her knee, face to face with herself, and touches with her forefinger the different parts of the child's face, mentioning thus the parts touched :—

> " Forehead bimper,
> Eye peeper,
> Nose snuffer,
> Cheek cherry,
> Mouth merry,
> Chin chopper."

Or the following may be said instead :—

> " Broo branty,
> Eye winky,
> Nose noppy,
> Mouth moppy,
> Chin choppy, and
> Kittly, kittly, kittly."

ending by tickling the child under the chin.

Or each part of the face is touched while saying the rhyme :—

> " Knock at door, *(brow)*
> Peep in, *(eye)*
> Lift up sneck, *(nose)*
> Walk in." *(mouth)*

A common rhyme for the hand or foot, is :—

> " This pig went to market, *(thumb or great toe)*
> This pig stayed at home, *(first finger)*
> This got some roast beef, *(second finger)*
> But this little pig got none, *(third finger)*
> And this went 'wee, wee, wee, wee,' *(little finger or toe)*
> All the way home."

The mother, taking the child's hands in hers, claps them together, saying :—

> " Clap a cake, clap a cake, baker's man,
> Make it and bake it, as fast as you can,
> Prick it and stick it, and mark it with D,
> And put in your oven for Dora and me."

The ensuing rhyme must be of considerable antiquity, dating before the introduction of tea and other modern beverages, and pointing to the time when "good ale" was the common drink. The child's hand is opened, and circles traced with the forefinger on the outstretched palm, repeating :—

> " Round about, round about, applety pie,
> Baby loves good ale, and so do I,

> Up mother, up, and fill us a cup,
> And baby and me will sup her all up."

The following is evidently a picture of life in the days of primitive man, when the produce of the chase formed food and clothing. Reading between the lines, we see that the tender flesh of the animal will be for the mother, though the warm fur furnishes a covering for the child.

> " Baby, baby, bunting,
> Father's gone a hunting,
> To get a little rabbit skin,
> To lap (wrap) baby bunting in."

The child being placed astride one foot of the nurse, which foot is raised from the ground through the leg being placed over the other, the following is repeated as the child is swung up and down, in imitation of riding.

> " Ride a cock horse, to Banbury Cross,
> To see little ——* get on a white horse,
> Rings on his fingers, and bells on his toes,
> He shall have music wherever he goes."

Or the following, with varied motion :—

> " This is the way the ladies ride, *(gently)*
> This is the way the farmers ride, *(quicker and higher)*
> This is the way the gentlemen ride." *(violently, so that the child may even be unseated)*

Here follow two counting-out rhymes, used by children to select one of their number, preparatory to a game. The boys say :—

> " Meeny, meeny, miny mo,
> I ax ya wheear mun this man go?
> Sum gans eeast, an' sum gans west,
> An' sum gans ower high crake nest."

> * Insert boy's name.

The girls chant the following :—

> " Eeny, meeny, miny mo,
>   Catalina, si-ne so,
>   Kay-o-way, Kitty-ca-lan,
>   Thou shalt be my soldier man,
>   To ride my horse, to beat my drum,
>   To tell me when my enemy come.
>   O. U. T. spells very fair,
>   Rottom, bottom, dish clout,
>   Out goes she."

A school-boy rhyme, addressed to those who come late to school, runs thus :—

> " Diller a dollar,
>   A ten o'clock scholar,
>   What maks yo' cum so soon ?
>   You used ti cum at ten o'clock,
>   Bud noo yo' cum at noon."

Should rain threaten to, or actually spoil sport, or a holiday, children chant :—

> " Rain, rain, go away !
>   Little Lily wants to play."

Or, being mindful only of the present, they say :—

> " Rain, rain, go away !
>   Come another washing day."

When, however, the rain does not interfere with their pleasure, their rhyme is :—

> " Rain, rain faster !
>   Coo's gone ti pasther." (pasture)

As a relic of the days when prayers were addressed to Saints, and as shewing the effect of the Reformation, the old invocation to " Matthew, Mark, Luke, and John," to " bless the bed I lie upon," has been altered to :—

> " Matthew, Mark, Luke and John,
>   Tak a stick and bray 'em on."

Of rhymes relating to times and seasons, the following may be cited. The storms which occur in February are often severe and destructive, so

"A Candlemas crack,
Ligs monny a sailor on his back."

The weather in early spring is thus characterised.

"February fill dyke,
Fill with black or white,
March muck it oot,
With a besom and a clout."

February is here represented as filling the ditches either with rain or snow water, and March follows with drying winds, and dries up the water, leaving the ditches clean and dry, as though they had been brushed out by a besom and dried with a cloth. The following rhyme introduces April and May :—

"March winds and April showers,
Bring forth May flowers."

APPENDIX A.

The Elder Edda tells how Thor's hammer was stolen by Thrym while Thor was asleep, and as this was a dreadful loss to both gods and men, its recovery was of supreme importance.

> " Wroth was King Thor
> When he woke from his rest,
> Felt for his hammer
> And found it was gone;
> Beard he gan bristle,
> Locks he gan lug,
> Earth's boy took to beating
> About with his fists."

Loki clad in Freyja's feather suit flew to Ogreland and found Thrym, the thief, and asked him if he had the hammer, for it fared ill with the gods and themselves.   Thrym quoth,

> " I have the Hardhitter's
> Hammer here hidden,
> Miles measured eight
> Deep down in mould.
> It now no man
> E'er may bring back,
> Save when he fetches me
> Freyja to wife."

Thor and Loki go to Freyja, and want her to carry out the arrangement.   She is angry and refuses.

> " Wanton and wedding sick
> Call thou this woman,
> If I drive with thee
> To Ogreland down."

A council was held, and it was decided to deceive Thrym by dressing someone else as Freyja.

> "Then they bound Thor
> In bridal array ;
> Clasped round his throat
> Brising's broad collar ;
> Down at his girdle
> The housewife's keys dangle ;
> Full round his knees, too,
> Women's weeds fall ;
> Broad stones and bright
> He bore on his breast ;
> Ay, and so tidily
> Topp'd up his head."

Loki went as waiting maid, and when the enormous appetite and flaming eyes of Thor caused remarks, he lulled suspicion by saying she had neither eaten nor slept for eight nights because of her eagerness to see "dear Ogreland." As the marriage could not be hallowed without the hammer, it was brought, and placed on the knee of the disguised bride.

> " Laughed then the Hardhitter's
> Heart in his breast,
> As hard-hafted hammer
> He handled again ;
> Thrym he slew first of all,
> Lord of the Thursa-kin ;
> Then all that Ogre-land
> Battered to bits.
>
> .   .   .   .
>
> .   .   .   .
>
> .   .   .   .
>
> So came at last
> Odin's son to his hammer."

Once A Week. 1861. p. 125.

APPENDIX B.

The following, by T. T. Wildridge, Esq., author of *Old and New Hull; Holderness and Hullshire Historic Gleanings,*

&c., was received too late for insertion in the proper place, but its value justifies its appearance here.

BARTHOLOMEW PRESTON, THE CHARMER, OF SWINE.

The horrors of witchcraft seem to have been the last great evil which with-stood the general enlightenment coming with the 17th century. Even now partial beliefs linger in dark corners of the East Riding, and much might be gathered concerning these existing relics of once flourishing superstitions. For a glimpse, however, at the full bloom of these various parasites of unhealthy faith in the supernatural, we must go back to the beginning of the reign of James I., or the last years of Queen Elizabeth, and no local example is so well supplied with details as the account of Bartholomew Preston, the Charmer, of Swine.

This notorious wizard was born at Wyton, East Yorks., probably in the reign of Elizabeth. His sister Margery was well-known as a bone-setter and midwife, and her skill gave rise to suspicions of dealings with unlawful spirits. She married a man named Ganton. After the death of old Margery, the cloak of suspicion of witchcraft fell upon Bartholomew, and without duly considering to what such a course might lead him, he encouraged the belief, stating that he had dealings with the fairies, and derived his power from them. He is said to have stated, to a man of Sutton, that he had intercourse with that kind of spirits. He was popularly credited with many curious faculties, and was much resorted to by people in any kind of trouble. Thus, if persons who had had anything stolen from them came within nine days he was able to tell them where the articles were, or, at any rate, give them some clue. Also, if any man's cow, horse, or any other beast was " forspoken " or witched, he was able, before he was informed, to tell him of what colour the stricken beast was. These and other similar displays of power gave him a great reputation throughout the district, and scarcely a village in Holderness but knew something of his wonderful abilities. He was much frequented by persons from Hull. An Alderman's wife was said to have great faith in him for the benefit he wrought in her sick son, and Barrick Newton, a butcher, often went over to consult him as to his (Newton's) wife, both using his services during many years. One Rowland Savage, a mariner, of Hull, also was one of his patients, as were many others of that town. In short, he was a quack who professed magic to help out a more or less extensive knowledge of the healing art.

Those were tender times, however, for such a man to make enemies, and he somehow managed to do it. He became looked upon as having gone beyond the legitimate intercourse with the unseen world. His enemies, according to the ordinary course of human nature, multiplied, and even his patients who had benefited, as well as others who had not, were ready to testify against him. John Ruksby, the miller, of Tunstall, offered to swear to his ability to tell the colour of charmed cows, saying he had often been with him, and made many trials of his skill in that kind of divination. John Thompson, of Lowthorpe, was ready to speak of stolen properties traced by his means. But the medical cases were the most severe. He was said to have witched to death a child he was called to attend in Hull, and John Wormsey, the father of the child, came to Swine with a warrant for his apprehension, the Deputy Constable of Swine, William Cob, being ready to execute it. Preston, however, made the matter up with the aggrieved father, and nothing more was heard of the matter till the other cases cropped up, and Wormsey, then a prisoner in the Hull Gaol for some offence, was referred to. Preston had also been sent for to attend a young man at Paull, who was "straungly visseted." It was affirmed against him in this case that he had merely tied a handkerchief round the young man's neck and assured his friends of his recovery. But when the charmer had gone, the young man cried out that "the rats which was on the handkerchief was lyk to kill him," and so he died. A boatman named Wintringham was ready to affirm the truth of this.

These reports were made to some local magistrates, but where, is not known, neither is the result of his trial, if he ever was brought to one. He was not the only charm doctor of his time, and it is possible an example was sought to be made of him. Remembering the pillory, the water ordeal and the blazing faggots round the stake, let us charitably hope he adopted the discreet course, and ran away.

T. T. W.

INDEX.

T. HOLDERNESS, PRINTER, DRIFFIELD,

www.ingramcontent.com/pod-product-compliance
Lightning Source LLC
Chambersburg PA
CBHW022354020726
47500CB00002B/269